Praise for *My Name*

Wonder is a wonder! This is a story that takes you to that .... .nt place we all loved during story time in our childhood. You can't wait to read the next chapter!

—Alicia Nicholson, Author, *21 Days of Loving You*

There are books you just want to linger over, and *My Name is Wonder* is one of those. Delightful, wonderful—and full of wonder.

—Barbara Steinbrenner

Like Ron Chapman's other books, I found *Wonder* to have multiple levels. On the surface, it is a light read, almost a children's story, about a little goat with a lot of curiosity. On another level, however, *Wonder* teaches us that we are not what and who we think we are, nor what others think of us; we are so much more—and less.

—Rosemary Parsells

Reading *Wonder* took me back to my childhood as a latchkey kid who came home from school to read and got lost in the characters and the adventure. It took me back to when I would forget to eat and had a flashlight under the bedcovers, thoroughly engrossed in the book.

—Charm Lindblad

My Name Is Wonder

Also by Ronald Chapman

A Killer's Grace (2012)
Seeing True: Ninety Contemplations in Ninety Days (2008)
What a Wonderful World: Seeing Through New Eyes (2004)

Audio Sets
Seeing True: The Way of Spirit (2016)
Breathing, Releasing and Breaking Through (2015)

My Name Is Wonder
A Tale of Adventure

Ronald Chapman

Terra Nova Books

SANTA FE, NEW MEXICO

Cover Illustration: "Rio Chama," used with permission of Jennet Inglis

Library of Congress Control Number 2016944137

Distributed by SCB Distributors, (800) 729-6423

Terra Nova Books

Published by Terra Nova Books, Santa Fe, New Mexico.
www.TerraNovaBooks.com

ISBN 978-1-938288-78-4

For Brianne and Natalie with fond memories of wonderful stories.

And with thanks to Richard Bach for planting a seed.

Where do shadows fall when there is only light?
—Mary Chapin Carpenter

CONTENTS

Part I

1

IN THE BARN

NANETTE GOAT LAY UPON THE SWEET-SMELLING HAY, HER sides heaving with the effort of her labor. William Goat, silent and strong, stood at her side. Though he had sired many kids, this was Nanette's first.

It was a beautiful winter morning, and though there was an arid chill in the air, the sun was climbing steadily into the iridescent blue sky. Its rays glittered golden upon the light dusting of snow that blanketed the world. Such mornings were common in the land that lay in the eastern lee of the mountains, but this one was special—at least to William and Nanette. As the light reached its fingers through the cracks in the barn's walls, their son was born.

Nanny would later say her son simply could not wait one moment longer if it meant missing the breaking day.

Propelled by a force as deep and ancient as life, the new mother curled herself around the kid. He was sleek and long-legged, slick from birth, and strangely silent. Instinctively, she licked him clean, and the gentle action of the long strokes of her tongue stimulated life force in the little goat.

He blinked—once, twice—and gazed around the strange place in which he had arrived.

In all his years and through numerous offspring, Willie had never seen a kid that did not bleat or squirm in its first minutes of life. This one lay on his side with head raised, eyes moving back and forth, surveying his surroundings. Nanny, her view perhaps colored by a mother's love, held that there had never been a hand-somer kid. He was pure white, with nary a spot on his soft coat.

As her first-born rolled onto his stomach, legs akimbo, and gazed straight up into his mother's face, she knew instinctively that he was a bright little fellow. He cocked his head in a curious sort of way, as if he found her both fascinating and a little puzzling.

Nanny murmured to herself, "Wonder."

Then she turned to Willie and announced, "We'll call him Wonder."

Like the many generations of goats that had preceded him, Willie always trusted a female's intuition, and he knew Nanny's name was perfect for his son. "Wonder it shall be," he said.

Now christened, little Wonder struggled to his feet only to topple immediately onto the straw. He looked at the ground as if surprised to find it there. It would not be the last tumble he would take. Nor would it be the last time that odd look of surprise lit up his face, a testament to both his name and his nature.

2

THE FAR MOUNTAINS

WONDER LOVED NOTHING BETTER THAN TO EXPLORE. LIKE all goats, he had the uncanny ability to escape any corral, fence, or paddock. It wasn't long before he acquired the nickname "Wander."

Gossip in the barnyard often focused on Wonder's exploits. Whenever Nanny would hear the hens clucking over his latest scrape or Mr. and Mrs. Mule muttering about his most recent mischief, she quickly corrected them. "Wonder is not mischievous! Why, that would suggest he intends to cause trouble." With a pleased gleam in her eyes, she would add, "Wonder is simply interested in everything he sees. It's his nature."

But in the quiet evenings when Wonder slept, Nanny confided her fears to Willie. Wonder wandered wherever he willed, and one day, she was sure, he would get hurt or lost—or worse. It was a big world, after all, and he was such a little goat.

Nanny, having recounted their son's latest misadventure, would ask, "Willie, what should we do with him?"

"Nanette," Willie would reply in his calm, stoic way, "let the kid be."

Nanny would roll her eyes in exasperation, but try as she might, she could never persuade Willie to take a firmer stance in Wonder's upbringing. He believed deeply in letting kids be kids. That was how Willie had been raised, as had his pappy before him, and his grandpappy, and all the way back through generations of proud he-goats. When his son came to him with a scraped nose or cockleburs all knotted up in his white hair, Willie would say, "Wonder, that which doesn't kill you will only make you stronger."

Wonder took the lesson to heart. Fearless and curious, he wandered ever farther. Whenever he got into trouble—which happened often—he would quietly whisper to himself, "Well, it didn't kill me."

Wonder was especially captivated by the jagged, purple mountains to the west. How far away were they? What did the grass taste like there? And what lay on the other side? Manuel, an older goat brought in from a Spanish herd that had once pastured in their shadows, affectionately called the mountains *Las Montañas Grandes*, a name that only added to their mystique for Wonder. He sometimes whispered the words to himself as he gazed at the horizon, not knowing that they meant only "big mountains."

The other goats of the herd were all weary of being pummeled by Wonder's endless questions. In truth, none of them had any first-hand knowledge of the mountains, yet that did not sway the certainty of their beliefs in the dangers that lurked among the jagged peaks. Legends told of distant, shaggy kin who scaled those rocky slopes, larger and more glorious than any ordinary goat. Some said they were direct descendants of the Gods from which all goats sprang. There were birds the size of barns up there too, and fierce, lithe creatures with sharp teeth and claws.

"It's no place for a young goat," the herd would say. "Get your head out of the clouds and keep your hooves on the ground."

Wonder vowed that someday, he would see those mountains for himself, climbing as far up as his legs would take him.

3

An Adventure by the Stream

ONE BRIGHT SPRING DAY, WONDER STOLE AWAY FROM THE herd, crawling under fences and through bushes to investigate the stream that cut through the lower pasture. He was so entranced by the burbling water and shiny, darting creatures he would later learn were fish that he lost track of time. Before he knew it, the day had passed and night was falling.

The little goat may have been fearless, but he did not want to spend the night alone, far away from the warmth and comfort of his herd. So he leaped up from the reeds beside the water and bounded across the pasture that separated him from the other goats.

It was not until he felt the sharp talons pierce his shoulders that Wonder realized he was in danger. He was being plucked from the earth and lifted up, up into the sky, and had it not been for the pain, he might have enjoyed the sensation of flight. Craning his neck, he looked up and saw the sharp, wickedly curved beak and yellow eyes of a great owl.

"Excuse me, sir," said Wonder, for Nanny had raised him to be a polite kid. "Would you mind putting me down?"

The owl flapped his wings and rose higher into the sky. Wonder could see a wide, wandering canyon leading westward. The distant mountains were lit as if by fire from the sinking sun. He had never seen Las Montañas Grandes from this angle before, and for a brief but interminable moment of awe, he forgot all about the pain in his shoulders.

Then out of the corner of his eye, Wonder glimpsed a black shape speeding toward them. The crow crashed into the owl just in front of its right wing. The owl dipped and wobbled but corrected his flight. The black bird wheeled around in a wide circle and dove again, this time from the left.

Weighed down by the goat, the owl could not easily maneuver, and the crow moved with speed and agility that seemed uncanny. He jabbered and squawked, hurling curses at his foe as he slashed with a sharp beak and wiry black feet. Each time the crow attacked, the owl would drop closer to the ground. The giant predator struggled to rise, but the ferocity of the crow simply would not permit it.

After what seemed like the longest time but could only have been moments, the owl relinquished its hold on the little goat. Wonder plummeted, his fall broken by a field of deep, sweet hay.

Wonder quickly scrambled to his feet, but not to flee. He watched breathlessly as the crow drove the owl from the pasture. The raptor flew away at last, and the black bird lit upon the branch of a tree by the stream. The goat cocked his head in puzzlement. Why had this stranger saved him? But before he could ask, he heard his mother's worried bleats carrying across the field.

Well, at least it didn't kill me, thought Wonder. His gaze swiveled between the crow and home. Inwardly he was torn. Should he run to meet Nanny, or should he return to the stream to investigate the mysterious crow?

It was the deep rumble of his father's call that decided the answer. Wonder took one last, reluctant glance at the crow. While the growing dusk made it difficult to see clearly, the crow seemed to lift its beak and rotate its head to focus a single beady eye on the goat. Wonder would have sworn the bird winked at him.

"Wonder!" called the gruff voice of William Goat once more. With a shake, Wonder raced toward home. He surprised himself when a single leap carried him over the fence into the upper pasture. He knew he could not jump high enough to clear that fence, and yet here he stood with his hooves planted in the familiar grass.

Any further thought was stifled as the goats closed ranks around him. He saw his father first, a look of relief—and perhaps even a little pride—on his long, narrow face. Then his mother butted through the crowd.

"You are in so much trouble, young goat," she said, her fear making the words sharp.

"But Maa—" he bleated, till she cut him off.

"What were you thinking? You could have been killed!"

"But Maa—" he tried again.

"Wonder, if you tell me that at least it didn't kill you, you *and* your father will both be in deep trouble." She paused and glanced from her son to his father—not missing the sparkle of approval in Willie's eyes. Nanny could tell he wouldn't be any help. The rest of the herd watched and muttered, but she knew they wouldn't weigh in either. None of them was foolish enough to get between a mother and her kid. At last, she said, "Well, what have you got to say for yourself?"

Wonder felt the weight of the herd's silence as they waited for him to answer. He looked down and dug at the turf for a moment before replying, "Maa, I'm sorry I scared you—but you wouldn't believe the view!"

Willie chuckled, the deep, resonant sound filling the night air. "Well said, son. Well said. Nanette, my love, those wounds of his need tending."

His mother shook her head and rolled her eyes, but she stepped forward and began to lick the wounds gently. Wonder leaned against her legs.

"You're trembling, son," she said quietly so only he could hear. "It must have been terribly frightening."

"Maa, I never thought to be afraid," he said.

Nanny cleaned the last of the blood from his shoulders and then nudged him with her nose. "No more adventures, little one," she said.

Wonder nodded absently and peeked around her legs toward the stream, but the mysterious crow had vanished in the twilight. Nanny followed her son's wide-eyed gaze beyond the pasture fence.

"At least not until you've healed," she sighed.

4

WOUNDED

WONDER AWOKE WELL AFTER SUNRISE THE NEXT DAY. Usually he was up with the dawn, but his limbs had stiffened in the night, and he felt sore and tired after his ordeal with the owl. He stretched and then moved gingerly from the barn. He hoped it would be no more than a few days before his wounds healed, but to a young goat as curious as Wonder, a few days seemed like an eternity.

He breathed deeply. It was an unusually beautiful day, or perhaps it only seemed so because he was, remarkably, alive to enjoy it. Wonder explored the pasture as if seeing it for the first time. The grass seemed greener and tasted sweeter, and he greeted even the gossipy chickens and dour Mr. and Mrs. Mule with enthusiasm.

Then he noticed the other goats staring at him.

Wonder wasn't very good at being a herd animal. He lacked the instincts that made the others band together, and the kid was most likely to keep to himself. Sometimes he thought it might be nice to have a little company, but his interest in the world was sufficient to provide endless entertainment.

Though he was content to be alone most of the time, Wonder was aware of the disquiet this caused others. Being quite bright, he noticed the gossip and odd looks that would fall in his direction. Now, after the unusual events of the previous day, those looks had grown stranger still.

Several kids his own age studied him from where they had gathered a short distance away. When they noticed him looking, they bleated nervously and shied. With a growing sense of discomfort, Wonder deliberately looked away and raised his gaze upward to the roofline of the barn. The kids followed his gaze. They nudged each other, whispering loudly, "You ask him." "No, you!"

Manuel, the cantankerous old goat from the Spanish herd, glared at the kids. *"Que pasa?"* he asked in an abrasive tone. "I'm trying to sleep."

One of the kids answered breathlessly, "Wonder sees something."

"Does he now?" sneered the old goat. "Eh, little buffoon, what's up?"

A nervous titter arose from the gathered kids.

Wonder turned, surprised by the vehemence with which Manuel had asked the question. He stammered slightly as he tried to conceal his discomfort, but he still addressed his elder politely. "I-I'm sorry, Master Manuel, I didn't hear you."

Manuel snorted. "Deaf too? I said, what are you looking at, buffoon?"

The situation bewildered little Wonder. He felt an ache in his belly that he would later come to recognize as embarrassment. Having never felt it before, he didn't know what to make of the sensation. "My name is Wonder, sir," he said.

"Wonder, huh? Your mama should have called you Fool's Goat. Fits better, eh?" Manuel champed his teeth and blew out a disgusted breath through his nose.

The kids gleefully whispered this new nickname to each other. "Fool's Goat, Fool's Goat!"

While Wonder knew that ruminant etiquette required him to reply to his elder, a sixth sense told him any answer he gave would lead to more mockery. The ache that had started in his belly spread throughout his body. Questions raced silently through his mind like dark clouds: *Why does Manuel hate me? And why do the others laugh?*

"There are some who think you special, Fool's Goat." Manuel snorted and shook his head. "Special indeed, *Idiota*," the old goat spat.

The comment was so ugly that the onlooking kids no longer tittered in amusement. They glanced away, apparently unwilling to meet the gaze of either Wonder or Manuel.

At that moment, an odd and disquieting feeling spread through Wonder. It was a little like embarrassment but colder and deeper in his bones. It was shame. *There is something wrong with me*, he thought. *That's why I'm not like the others.*

Wonder blinked away tears. He remembered his mother's urgings to settle down and spend time with the herd, the fleeting comments made by the other kids, and the suspicious, judgmental looks of his fellow goats. He *wasn't* like them, and he suddenly realized that being different might be a bad thing. A terrible lump grew in Wonder's throat.

For the first time in his young life, he had no idea what he should do.

5

OREN

OUT OF THE CORNER OF HIS EYE, WONDER SAW OLD OREN angling across the yard toward them. He was a very wise buck, much revered by everyone. Wonder had not talked with him before; the elderly goat kept to himself in his own corner of the paddock. Though he was white-faced with age and walked with a careful, doddering step, his eyes were keen. Those eyes were watching Wonder.

Shaken by his troubling thoughts and feelings, Wonder nonetheless stepped forward and said respectfully, "Good day, Master Oren. I'm Wonder, son of William and Nanette Goat." He bowed down so that his nose touched the turf, ignoring the pain in his shoulders.

The wise goat stopped in front of the gathered herd. "Hmmphf," he grumbled. A long pause followed. Then Oren slowly pivoted and lowered his baleful gaze at Manuel.

"Now, you wouldn't be harassing little Wonder, would you?" asked Oren in a deep, resonant voice.

A mischievous look crossed the Spanish goat's face before he responded. "Only offering a few pointers."

"With the best of intentions, no doubt." Oren laughed heartily, and his white beard shook. "You may go now, Manuel."

Something in Oren's demeanor made it quite clear they were all dismissed. Manuel and the kids quickly scattered.

Oren turned back to Wonder and spoke gently. "First, little one, I must tell you that you are *not* Wonder."

Wonder knew enough about Oren to know he spoke with the weight of the wisdom of generations. He had also heard that Oren was a philosopher. The gravity of the moment was not lost on the little goat as he considered this statement carefully. Somehow he knew that nothing but the truth would suffice.

"I don't get it," he said with a scrunched up face.

"Your name may be Wonder, but Wonder you are not." He studied the kid, watching for any signs of dawning comprehension. Wonder cocked his head to one side, still puzzled, and the old buck continued. "The form you find yourself in is that of a goat, but you are not a goat. There is that which is, and then there is that which is truth. If you are to learn, you must learn to be absolutely clear about such matters."

Oren fell silent, waiting.

Wonder blinked—once, twice—and then said, "Got it!"

The wise goat responded in an amused tone, "Do you now?"

"Yes, sir. My name is Wonder." He grinned and then continued, "And I am not that."

"Ha!" responded Oren. "I believe you do have it, young one, but let us see." He almost, but not quite, grinned back at Wonder. It was hard to tell with the long, white beard. "What are you if not Wonder?"

The kid leaped at the answer. "Well, sir, I don't guess I know."

"Indeed," replied Oren, his yellow eyes dancing. "True wisdom is knowing that you know nothing."

"Then I must be very wise indeed, sir."

Oren chuckled. "Let us try this idea and see what you make of it. What you *are* is what is left when that which is not you is cast aside."

Wonder frowned, trying to puzzle it out. A light of understanding dawned in his eyes, and he bounced in the grass delightedly, but just as suddenly as it had appeared, it dimmed and was hidden again, like a cloud passing in front of the sun.

"I can see that you understand, but sometimes understanding slips away," said Oren. "Let this be your first lesson, and listen well:

Each of us becomes our own identity. If I asked you to describe yourself to me now, you might say that you are a small, white-coated goat with a predilection for adventure. We create a composite image from these bits and pieces—the color of our eyes, the size of our horns—but when we attach the meaning of ourselves to being a goat or a duck or a hog, we mistake ourselves. Do you follow me, Wonder?"

Wonder nodded attentively. An insect buzzed past his ear, and he flicked it away without so much as a thought, so riveted was he by Oren's words.

"You are none of these things. Nor are you the name you have been given. Take them away, and what is left is the real you."

"I-I think I understand, Master Oren, sir," said Wonder.

"Let us dispense with formalities. I am Oren, which is what you may call me."

"No, sir," Wonder countered.

Oren lifted his head, a gleam in his eye. "And why would that be, Wonder?"

The kid laughed and rolled onto his back, waving his legs in the air. "Because you are not Oren! That is just your name."

"Aha!" exclaimed the old one. "Your father said you were bright, and I see that it is so. Many years ago, I answered my old master exactly as you did."

Wonder sat up. "My father talked to you about me?"

"William asked me to teach you," said Oren. "Did he not tell you?"

The little goat shook his head. "No, sir. I mean, Oren."

"Well, now you know," the goat finished curtly. "I will expect you each afternoon shortly after midday sleep."

"Oren?" Wonder asked tentatively.

"Yes, little one?"

"I kind of get into a lot of trouble," the kid admitted.

"Is that so?"

"Well, everything is so interesting . . . and it seems like every time I go to investigate, something unexpected happens."

Oren chuckled. "Curiosity and trouble are fine ways to learn, Wonder. They will serve you well."

Oren turned and walked slowly toward William and Nanette, who stood together across the yard, watching their son.

The other members of the herd were also watching. Wonder felt a twist of doubt in his belly again, but he breathed deeply, steeling himself, and met their gaze. His daddy-goat thought Wonder was bright, and old Oren was to be his teacher. He had nothing to be ashamed of. After a moment, the other goats looked away or became very interested in cropping the grass at their feet. Wonder walked triumphantly toward the hay rack—or as triumphantly as he could while limping.

6

The Return of the Crow

Wonder began his education the next day under the patient tutelage of old Oren. It was not quite what the kid had expected, with long periods of quiet reflection interspersed with Oren's simple observations.

"Look, Wonder," Oren said. "There goes Lucius. Do you see how he behaves in order to gain the attention of the other young bucks?"

And Wonder dutifully looked at Lucius, a swaggering goat with black and tan markings who was scraping his horns against the side of the barn.

Later, Oren said, "Wonder, can you guess why daily gossip is so important to the nannies who sometimes gather in the far corner of the pasture?"

And Wonder watched the she-goats gossiping as they cropped the turf.

"Wonder, the wind has shifted to the north, and light clouds are moving before it. Do you think it will rain?"

The kid simply listened and watched and waited. He knew it was not his place to initiate. Finally Oren said, "Few goats can speak of being aloft. Tell me of your flight."

Wonder told his teacher about the lazy afternoon by the stream and of the strange, silver creatures he had found there. Oren told him they were called "fish," and were not good to eat. Then he motioned for Wonder to continue.

Wonder was so absorbed in describing the aerial battle between the crow and the owl that he failed to notice when Oren's attention shifted away.

"Look, little one," said Oren, interrupting Wonder's blow-by-blow account.

"Your crow has come to join us. Perhaps he hopes to hear of his noble deed."

Wonder twisted his head to follow Oren's gaze. There was the crow perched atop a fencepost. Wonder nodded in greeting, and the crow bobbed its head.

Wonder noticed that the crow's right eye socket was calloused over from a long-ago wound. He pointed this out to Oren.

"That is unusual enough, but so too is the shabbiness of his feathers." The old goat chuckled. "Perhaps he aspires to the appearance of his cousin, the ruffled grouse."

"CRAACK!" The crow's call was so sudden and loud that it made Wonder tumble to the grass. He looked up and saw the crow shuffling from foot to foot and flapping his wings in irritation.

"My apologies, Master Crow," said Oren with a hint of amusement in his voice. "But one must always be sure of the company one keeps. Will you speak with us?"

The crow stared at them with its one good eye, blinked, and then settled more comfortably atop the post.

"Very well," said Oren. "Keep your own counsel, if you wish." The old goat shifted his focus back to his student. "You've described the particulars of your short time in the air, but I'd like to know what you felt."

Wonder tore his gaze from the crow. "Well, Maa thought I should have been frightened, but honestly, I wasn't scared. The talons hurt a lot at first, but as soon as I saw the canyon and the mountains beyond, I just stopped thinking about anything. It's like I forgot who and where I was. Then the fall was so quick and startling; I don't remember anything until I found myself scrambling to my feet. It was all very . . . surprising." He paused. "Oren, it was really fun," he admitted.

"And yesterday, when Manuel called you names—how did that make you feel?"

Wonder dropped his gaze. He hadn't known that Oren had seen his humiliation, and the thought made him feel like he'd just swallowed a slug. Tears welled up in his eyes, and he cleared his throat to dislodge the slug-lump of shame.

When Wonder did not answer, Oren said kindly, "I can see you were wounded. Manuel's cruel words hit hard, perhaps more painful than the owl's talons. Can you describe your feelings?"

Wonder did not want to return to that moment in his memory, but he did as his teacher asked. "I doubted myself. And I felt like something was wrong with me," he said as he stared miserably at the ground.

Oren nodded at Wonder's words and then looked again toward the bird. "Master Crow, feel free to join us any time you like. I do not know your purpose, but I share Wonder's curiosity about you."

The old goat watched the crow pick at his wiry black foot for a few moments. When it became clear the bird had nothing to say, he returned his attention to Wonder.

"Thank you for sharing your feelings with me, Wonder. And I'm proud that you admitted both your doubt and your delight. Enjoying ourselves may be the only thing that matters, but sometimes old goats like Manuel get enjoyment from taking away the happiness of others. We'll discuss this more at a later date. But I will say this: There is nothing to fear. Remember this always."

Oren studied the little goat's face, his wise yellow eyes seeming to look through him, before nodding again as if in approval. "So it is good that you had fun with your adventure in flight. And it is likewise good that you so readily felt the pain of your encounter with a jaundiced old goat. Now let us be quiet while I contemplate our feathered friend."

Wonder and Oren rested side by side in the grass, quietly watching the crow, while overhead the wind moved the clouds across the sky. Wonder tried to be as still as Oren, but it was hard not to fidget. The crow seemed unconcerned with their scrutiny. He preened his feathers—not that it did much good—and pecked at the top of the post where he sat, all the while watching the goats with his one beady eye.

At last, Oren said, "We are done for today, Wonder. I will see you tomorrow. And if I'm not mistaken, the crow will be joining us as well."

7

QUIET AND QUESTIONS

SEASONS PASSED, AND THE LITTLE WHITE GOAT GREW INTO A sturdy but smallish buck. Except for Oren and his parents, Wonder spent little time with the other goats. Sometimes he still heard the name "Fool's Goat," but as Wonder's misadventures were forgotten and he ceased to be quite so much of a novelty, the herd lost interest in him. He still avoided Manuel, however, and the old Spanish goat would not dare bully Wonder while he was with Oren.

It seemed to Wonder that Oren taught him very little. Sometimes the old buck hardly spoke at all. When he did speak, it was to make observations about the pasture and its inhabitants. Oren peppered these musings with questions, but as best as Wonder could tell, it didn't matter whether he answered them or not.

While there was no apparent pattern to Oren's teachings—if, in fact, they were teachings at all—the crow reliably joined them two or three times a week. Oren would cordially welcome the bird and then continue with the day's lesson. Sometimes he would try to include the crow, as on this day, some months after Wonder began his tutelage under Oren, when the old buck lifted his shaggy head and inhaled deeply.

"Ah, little one, can you smell the peaches ripening? Summer's heat makes them sweeter. When the time comes, perhaps we can discover the means to taste the fruit." Oren turned and locked his gaze on Wonder. "Do you remember how to jump the fence?"

he asked with a gentle smile. "Or perhaps Master Crow might fly out to the orchard and fetch us a peach. What do you say, O Feathered One?"

The bird uttered not a word.

Every now and again, Wonder was aware that he was changing—not just growing bigger, although he was certainly doing so, but somehow getting bigger on the inside too. He felt as though he understood things in a new way, a deeper way. Yet he could not fathom the source of this knowledge since it was obviously not introduced by Oren.

Wonder did not often ask questions during his lessons, but he wanted to know more about this strange new way of seeing the world. "Oren, I saw my father in a staredown with Manuel yesterday. I may have imagined it, but I knew exactly what they were thinking." Wonder cleared his throat. "How can I know that?"

The old buck studied Wonder thoughtfully for a moment and then resumed gazing up at the sky. At last, he said, "The canyon jays are bluer than I've seen them in some time. Do you suppose the darker blue of the juniper berries is the cause? Maybe more rain has caused them both to appear more blue. Or perhaps it is merely coincidence."

And that was all the answer Wonder was to get on the subject.

8

CHANGES IN THE WIND

IT WAS ON A WINDY AFTERNOON IN EARLY SPRING THAT OREN asked Wonder the question that would change the little goat's life. The day was cold, with winter yet holding on, but the sun was bright as it occasionally flickered behind thin clouds blown before the gusts.

"Can one say there is a purpose to anything, little one?" asked Oren.

They both sat quietly for a moment, watching the sky. A rustling noise announced the arrival of the crow. Wonder glanced upward to see the bird at his usual perch.

"You can answer me, Wonder," said the old goat. "What do you suppose has been the purpose of our time together?"

Wonder blinked in surprise. "Oren, you *never* ask me for an answer."

The teacher looked kindly upon his student. "Indeed, but I do now. What do you think?"

The little goat relaxed into the question and the quiet, thinking deeply. Minutes passed before he replied. "When I found out you were to be my teacher, I thought you'd be asking me questions and telling me the answers, that I'd be memorizing things and taking tests. Instead . . . you've just let me learn."

"A very wise answer, Wonder," said Oren. "Why have I never provided answers to you?"

Wonder glanced at the crow, who was watching them silently as he always did. "I've thought a lot about this," he said, "and I think it's because the answers are already inside me."

"Indeed," said Oren solemnly. "Everything there is to know or understand lies within us. It appears through our feelings as well as our intuition. But we become distracted by our lives. We forget our own inner knowing and fall into a walking sleep. Before long, we forget that we ever knew at all."

Oren glanced away into the distance. "Do you understand?"

Wonder nodded with a somber look on his face. He thought of the nannies gossiping in the clover, of the young bucks his own age endlessly posturing and showing off their horns.

"Good," continued his mentor. "To stay awake, you must remain attentive and curious about your surroundings, but you must also be still. Over and over again we notice, question, and become quiet. And answers come."

"That's exactly how it's been for me!" said Wonder. "The answers just show up, completely unannounced, if I pay attention to my thoughts and feelings."

Oren chuckled. "Yes, little one. If I had provided answers, you would have stopped listening within yourself. Giving them to you would have done nothing more than lull you back to sleep," Oren said. Then he added wryly, "As a teacher, I can easily add to your sleepiness."

The goats laughed at Oren's jest, and the crow jabbered. After a moment, the old buck became serious again. "Hear me well, Wonder. There is no better guide, and no better tool, than quiet reflection. Let your inner voice be your one, true guide. Learn to trust it, and it will never fail you. That is what's left when you cast aside all that is not you, all that is external to you or has its source from outside yourself."

"RAWWK!"

The gravelly, raucous squawk startled them both, and they turned to look at the crow. He turned his beady black eye on them, and to Wonder's amazement, he spoke at last.

9

THE CROW SPEAKS

GOOD WISDOM, OLD OREN. IT BECOMES YOU. PERHAPS IT IS you, nay?" The crow cackled to himself and then continued. "Long listened. Most pleased. Good counsel, good wisdom. Good Wonder!"

Wonder blinked at the bird. He'd grown used to the untidy bird's presence, but until now, Wonder had thought him to be deaf, mute, or perhaps both. Now, he said the only thing he could think to say. "You can talk!"

The crow bobbed its head. "Talk I can," he said. His voice was rough and hoarse but full of amusement.

"But . . . why have you never said anything before?" asked Wonder.

"Naught to say," cawed the crow. He swept his gaze from Wonder to Oren and back again. "Master Crow, you call me. Not my name, though master I am." A rough laugh followed as he stared at Wonder. "Mac Craack Crow is my name. But I like Master Crow better." A short burst of staccato caws punctuated the crow's amusement. "M.C. better still!"

Wonder tried to follow the crow's odd way of speaking. "So, Mast. . . I mean, M.C., why *did* you save me from that owl?"

The crow flapped his wings, sending his already-ruffled feathers into further disarray. "No answer, Wonder. No need to unteach. Wisdom from an old goat is wisdom indeed. What think you, ay?"

Oren laughed before Wonder could say anything further. "Mac Craack—or Master Crow if you prefer—I am delighted you shall allow Wonder to continue to be the source of his own wisdom. I am pleased to see such wisdom in you as well."

The crow nodded deferentially.

Oren nodded back and said, "However, I am an old goat, and I hope that you'll indulge me with an answer. Why have you at last chosen to speak with us, Master Crow?"

"Hmmm . . . what does Wonder think? Or feel?"

Wonder didn't say anything at first. Then he realized both Oren and Mac Craack were looking at him expectantly. "Oh," he began with a laugh, "I'm so used to just listening, I didn't think to answer." His head cocked to one side as he searched his thoughts and feelings. "It's not a coincidence that you saved me from the owl that night." A moment of stillness passed, broken only by the rushing of the wind, as Wonder listened for inner clarity. He felt certainty rise. "The reason you've been silent so far is because you've been waiting for me to learn that there is only the inner knowing. And now I know."

"CRAACK," replied Mac Craack. "Wise young goat too! The voice inside speaks true, nay? Despite goats. Despite crow. Not I, not I, not I."

Oren guffawed and stamped his hoof against the turf. "Not I, indeed, Master Crow!"

Wonder laughed along with them, although he wasn't entirely sure he got the joke.

"Mac Crow Craacked Master . . . AWWWK!" The crow laughed loudly. "No question. No answer. One question. New words, new answer. Not I."

Wonder giggled at the riddling of the crow, which made no sense to him. The bird turned to look upon the little goat.

"Laugh at Craacked Crow?"

"Not I!" said Wonder, and both Oren and M.C. burst into laughter once more. The sun seemed to grow warmer for a moment, and a gentle breeze stirred their hair and feathers. When their laughter subsided at last, they slipped into a comfortable silence.

The quiet was broken by the old goat. "Wonder, intuition tells me that you and Master Crow have come together for a purpose. Do you share that sense, or is it only the imaginings of an old goat?"

Before his student could reply, M.C. croaked, "Goat teach. Now I teach. Lucky Wonder!"

Wonder bowed his head, overwhelmed with a profound sense of gratitude. That two such wise creatures would spend their time teaching him made him feel quite humbled, but he was also sad that his lessons with Oren were coming to an end. The crow and Oren both turned their attention to him.

"Oren," Wonder began but broke off as his throat tightened with emotion. He tried again, "Oren, you're right. I know why Mac Craack has come. But I feel so much appreciation for you and for all that you've . . . ." Wonder choked up again.

Oren looked gently to the young goat. "Wonder, listen carefully to me. The gratitude you felt for me just now is what I have felt for you all along. There is no teacher without a student, and thus no teaching. We have learned together, and it has been my pleasure to do so with you."

Quiet embraced them like an old friend. It was the sort of quiet that spoke volumes, if one only listened attentively. The trio waited as the presence washed over them and then slowly waned.

Wonder listened, and he realized what he must do next. He turned to the crow. "M.C., I am going to the mountains. That's been my wish for so long. I can't tell you why, but you are to go with me."

"Craacked young goat!" chortled M.C. "Need a whack? A whack to the head, nay?"

Wonder shook his head. "No, thank you. But . . . I do need a guide."

The crow bobbed his head, his single eye agleam. "Craacked travel. None better. Mac Craack will go."

And so Wonder's lessons with Oren came to an end, and his new journey began.

10

PLANS IN THE MAKING

AS THE WEATHER CONTINUED TO WARM, THE TRIO CHATTED each day, planning for Wonder's trip to the mountains. Though Oren was no longer Wonder's teacher, their time was still filled with long periods of silence peppered by the old buck's observations.

One beautiful afternoon, when the scent of wildflowers wafted on the wind, Mac Craack announced, "Fine smells and green sights. Craacked travel time is nigh!"

Wonder felt a rush of anxiety and anticipation. Although he was perhaps too old to do so any more, he bounced on the turf like a kid and cried, "Really? When do we leave? Oh, I can't wait!"

"One thing we must do," said the crow. "Master Oren, time to talk of Fool's Goat?"

Shame shot through Wonder, slithering like a cold snake through his insides, at the sound of the nasty name.

The old goat replied softly, "Yes, Master Crow, we must speak with our little one about that episode. The time has arrived."

Oren carefully scrutinized his protégé's face before beginning. "Wonder, this world little understands the inner realm you've come to know so well. Worse, fear causes others to attempt to squelch it in everyone else."

Oren became quiet, and a look of immense sadness welled up in his yellow eyes. A few moments later, he continued. "The great tragedy is that those efforts are usually successful. And yet, it is there that everything we seek is to be found. Contentment. Satisfaction. Peace. Security. All these lie within."

"GRAWK," interjected M.C. "Wounds hurt. Wounds make more wounds. Hurt makes hurt."

Oren nodded at the crow deferentially and then looked back toward the little goat.

"Wonder, Manuel is not a happy goat. He was indeed cruel to you, as others had been cruel to him, and so on and so on. The wound it left cannot be healed by anything I or Master Crow might say. Only you can heal it. No one but you can create your path. It lies on the outside, which is nothing but a mirror of the inside. But when you arrive, you'll know because the wound will no longer hurt. And in that moment you will feel nothing but compassion for yourself and for others."

"Long walk . . . large life . . . all good. Craacked good!" the crow added.

The little goat considered this for a while. "Then it is time to tell my parents that I'm leaving," he said at last.

"CAW, CAW, CAW!" sang M.C. *Viva la resistance!*

Wonder smiled, puzzled, as he gazed at the crow, who was hopping from foot to foot and flapping his wings. "Resistance?"

Oren ignored the crow's antics. "Little one," he said somberly, "the path to healing is filled with obstacles. It is difficult. Yet the obstacles and the resistance are the way."

Wonder's smile turned to a frown. "I think I'm ready. I *am* ready."

Oren gazed down at his former student lovingly. "Indeed you are."

"Thank you for every. . . ." Wonder began.

A throaty call erupted from Mac Craack. "CROCK! Resistance is crock. Craacked too! Only way out is through!"

11

Saying Farewell

WONDER TOLD HIS FATHER FIRST. AS HE APPROACHED THE trough where the older buck was enjoying a drink, he went over what he would say again and again. He waited until William finished his drink and then bowed in greeting. When he straightened, he was surprised to find that he no longer had to crane his neck quite so far to look up into his father's eyes.

"Hello, Father," said Wonder. So far, so good. "I, er, wanted to tell you . . . that is, I *need* to tell you that I'm going on a quest. To the mountains. With the crow."

Wonder felt himself making a muddle of things despite his carefully planned speech. He took a deep breath and tried again. "Father, I'm leaving. Not today but soon. I have to see what's beyond the fences."

He explained about the arrival of Mac Craack and the end of his lessons, and described as best he could the feelings that drew him toward the distant mountains. William listened silently, but although he said nothing, his eyes were awash with emotion. Finally, the buck assented with a single nod of his head.

"Wonder, you must do what calls to you," said William. "I trust Oren's guidance—even if I can't fathom this crow."

"Thank you," said Wonder.

"I'm very proud of you, son . . . and if you need me to talk to your mother, I will."

The younger goat basked in William's approving gaze, but after a long moment, he said, "Paa, I know Maa won't be happy, but I have to tell her."

His father laughed. "I'm sure if she doesn't kill you, it will only make you stronger."

Wonder joined him in his laughter. They stood quietly together, side by side for quite a while. Then Wonder knew it was time to find Nanny. He thanked his father again and purposefully strode across the yard. He found his mother lying in the sun with closed eyes, slowly chewing her cud. She opened her eyes as she heard him approach.

It was a difficult conversation, but Wonder was prepared. Nannette Goat had a knack for managing things to her liking, but not this time. Wonder repeated what he'd told William—although this time without the false start—and braced himself for the inevitable argument. He remained steadfast, and in the end, she admitted, "Oh, Wonder, somehow I know you will be fine. But I'm just a selfish nanny who doesn't want to give up her son . . . ever!"

Wonder knelt and pressed close to his mother. Then he turned with misty eyes and said gently, "Love you, Maa. And thank you."

A sigh rose from deep within her as she closed her eyes and leaned her head against her son's.

Word of Wonder's trek swept quickly through the herd. The odd looks and whispering returned full force. Manuel tried to provoke him with nasty remarks, and although Wonder felt the tinges of shame and anger rise, he did not respond. Oren had encouraged him to take the high road, to neither provoke nor reply, and Manuel soon lost interest and went in search of easier prey.

As Wonder prepared for his journey with the help of Oren and Mac Craack, some of the younger goats became interested, pretending to play nearby while they listened in with wide, shining eyes. In the evenings, the older goats would come up to Wonder, one by one, and offer advice or stories from their wild youths. The nanny goats mobbed him as a group, warning him of all the ills that could befall a goat who left the pasture. Wonder felt the weight of the herd's dreams and stories and fears, and he found that he was proud to carry them.

One afternoon, a doe his own age approached Wonder and told him of a dream she'd had about evil creatures who lived in a bend of the upper stream. They were sly, she said, and not to be trusted. She went on to tell him the name that had come to her in her dream: "Waters of the Others." As she uttered it, her voice fell to a whisper infused with fear and foreboding.

Wonder had heard many such tales, and it sounded to him like just another variation on the endless stories of trolls, giant serpents, and firebirds. Still, he thanked her for the warning.

Just before parting, the doe added, "Oh, and if you find the goats of the mountains, do come back and tell us of them! I hear they are magnificent!"

Wonder patiently assured her he would do just that. His smile had the desired effect, and she at last returned to her friends who lay nearby in the sun-dappled clover. Later that day when he met with Oren, he recounted the story. Oren admitted that what lay upstream was beyond his knowing. What was true would simply have to reveal itself. And like it or not, Wonder would have to deal with that truth.

Oren looked to M.C., sitting upon his fencepost. "Master Crow, what did you see in your flights today?"

Mac Craack replied, "Snow melt ends. Good sky. Time for Wonder to wander!"

12

UPSTREAM

WONDER AWOKE VERY EARLY THE NEXT MORNING, HIS thoughts and emotions filled with anticipation as he waited for dawn. It seemed to take hours for the sun to rise, but at last it did, and with it woke Wonder's parents. The little goat followed them out into the yard, and they greeted the day together, each knowing that it would be a long time before they did so again. Few words were uttered. Nanny wept softly. William offered to walk to the fence with him.

Wonder and his father were halfway across the pasture before the rest of the herd had awakened. As the dawn broke and the mist eased away, the morning proved to be clear and cool, ripe with the lovely promises of summer. Oren was already waiting for them at the fence, staring silently to the West. Mac Craack fluttered from post to post, seemingly unable to perch on any one of them for more than a few seconds.

When Wonder and his father joined them, the crow said curtly, "Go we must."

Oren, whose manners were much more refined, greeted William with the proper courtesy between two bucks of equal standing in the herd. Then he turned to Wonder. "Now it is time for you to go forth to find yourself. Remember, it is nothing that must be added to you, but that which is left when all that is not you has fallen away."

Both Oren and William nuzzled Wonder's face and then quickly turned and walked away to a respectful distance. They bowed low, their horns nearly brushing the turf. Wonder knew the gesture acknowledged him as a fellow buck, no longer a kid, and that it set him free to go.

Mac Craack lifted into the air with a brilliant, ringing cry. Wonder sprang, soaring over the fence to land lightly in the lower pasture. He turned for one last look at his home, his father, and his mentor. Then the excitement of the trek seized him. He whirled around and darted down the slope toward the stream. He saw M.C. a little distance ahead, flapping like a torn black flag, and Wonder galloped to meet him.

Their path unfolded with ease that first day. Wonder paced himself, alternating a trot with a steady walk, while Mac Craack swooped ahead to survey their route and then doubled back to give directions. The banks of the stream were rich with grasses and delectable shrubs, perfect for intermittent grazing and the occasional rest. Its waters were crisp and invigorating, whether to drink or to refresh legs that grew tired as the day wore on.

Other than the occasional directive, Mac Craack spoke little, and the trek became almost a walking meditation for Wonder. The floor of the valley remained even as the stream wound westward, but the goat noticed that the land rising to the sides varied greatly. Sometimes, the canyon walls pushed upward; other times, they rose in gentle, undulating slopes. At one point, they rested in a narrow passage where sandstone spires of burnished orange rose above them in breathtaking beauty. It would be the first of many sights the goat wished to never forget.

As the day drew to a close, Mac Craack led Wonder to a dense bramble that would provide cover for the night. Several rabbits burst forth in surprise at the novel sight of a goat burrowing deeply into their home. They would later return after determining he was no threat. But by then, Wonder had already fallen into a weary but contented sleep.

The tired young goat slept deeply until well after sunrise, then awoke disoriented. Quickly shaking away the confusion—and a number of leaves and twigs—he stumbled out of the brush and tripped. Wonder quickly picked himself up, but his crow companion had seen the tumble. Mac Craack cackled raucously from a nearby roost. "Sleepyhead goat. GRAACK! Escapegoat flies from brambles! GAW, GAW, GAW."

Wonder laughed at the familiar but mystifying banter. "Good morning, Master Crow. How did you rest?"

"Rest? With goat snoring like whole herd, nay?"

The goat shook his head in amusement. "Oren told me to make no attempt to reason with you, M.C."

"CRAACK! Master Crow is more Craacked than Mac, ay?"

"No more wisecracks, crow," Wonder said. "Not until I've had my breakfast."

The crow launched upward and flew away as Wonder settled into grazing and browsing. A short time later, they were under way. The steady motion helped to melt the soreness from his muscles as Wonder and Mac Craack made their way westward up the valley.

13

WATER OF THE OTHERS

THE FOLLOWING DAYS WERE MUCH THE SAME AS THE FIRST. While it was a comfortable routine with much to see, Wonder began to feel restless. Even when the valley opened up at just the right angle to offer a stunning glimpse of the mountains, the goat was surprised—and a little frustrated—that the snowcapped peaks appeared no closer.

Wonder called out to Mac Craack, "How much farther to the mountains?"

"So close. So far. Who knows? RAWWK!"

Despite the restlessness he felt, Wonder could not help but laugh as he replied, "Master Crow, you're hopeless!"

"It is what it is. Can't be more. Or less." The crow's words faded as he soared away.

As if in response to Wonder's desire for excitement, a massive line of late afternoon thunderstorms boiled up on the horizon and soon began to pelt them with rain. Mac Craack guided the goat toward higher ground, and Wonder took shelter in the undergrowth beneath an overhang.

He settled in to wait out the storm, but Mac Craack hopped out once he saw the goat was settled, and took to the sky.

"Wait," cried Wonder. "Don't you want to shelter from the storm? There's plenty of room for both of us."

Mac Craack swooped down and alit a few feet away from the overhang. He cocked his head and looked at Wonder for a moment. "Storm good," he croaked. "But wet goats bad. Mac Craack must go greet wind and rain. Old friends for an old crow, nay?"

Just before the crow departed, Wonder thanked him and joked, "I didn't want this kind of adventure!"

"CRAACK! Prayer is every word. Wonder should wonder." And with that the crow flew off again.

It proved to be a long and difficult night. Unrelenting, the rain fell until early morning. With the thunder, lightning, and wind, even the sheltering rock was poor cover. When finally Wonder slept, he had a terrible and terribly realistic dream. He saw from afar the barn and the goat herd. Men had come and were separating some of the goats to take them away. Horrified, Wonder watched helplessly as Oren was culled, though his mentor met the event with a peaceful and quiet countenance.

Wonder tried to move or to call out, but to no avail. As the goats were loaded, the scene began to fade, and he awoke with a loud bleat, his sides heaving with panicked breaths.

It was dawn. M.C. had not yet arrived from his evening roost. Wonder wanted to rush home immediately, but he forced himself to remain calm until his companion returned. When the crow finally arrived, Wonder blurted out that he had dreamed something was wrong with the herd and that Oren was in danger.

Mac Craack flew down and landed on a nearby branch. He cocked his head and looked into the goat's face with his one eye.

"Resist this resistance," he said in his gruff, gravelly voice.

"But Mac Craack—"

"GRAWWK! Wonder, breathe! Breathe in now. NOW!"

And Wonder breathed under the unflinching stare of the crow. Each time he tried to speak, the crow would simply utter, "Now is now. Inside is truth. Breathe. Listen. Feel."

Slowly, calm returned, but with it came tears of grief. Finally Mac Craack said, not unkindly, "What could have been was. Choose now. No forward. No back. Now."

"I want to go back, Mac Craack."

"Only now, young one. No choice to be made."

Wonder tipped his head and peered at the crow. "Okay. Then I'd like to drink and eat a little."

M.C. opened his beak to speak but paused. "Wonder wondering again. Good. Didn't kill him."

Wonder chuffed in strained amusement. Then he turned and plodded toward the stream, which was running deeper and murkier after the storm. The crow steered him to where the waterway turned sharply north and spread into a broad pool. A sloped and muddy path led to the edge of the water. Mac Craack announced that he must check the route and would return shortly.

Wonder moved slowly to the water's edge, turned his body slightly upstream where it was less muddied, and bent to drink. The water soothed. His mind no longer raced, but the flood of emotions had left him feeling slightly off balance.

An instant later, a squeal suddenly pierced the air. Before Wonder could look up, his legs were driven from beneath him and he plunged into the stream. The goat floundered for a moment before finding his footing and pulling himself to the shallows. He scanned the stream and bank but saw nothing. Puzzled, he shook himself, and water flew from his coat.

When he opened his eyes, he saw two furry heads peering at him from just above the surface, only a few feet away. Wonder blinked. The pair of eyes on the left blinked back at him. Wonder tilted his head to the side. The head on the right mimicked him.

On the edge of Wonder's vision, a motion on the bank caught his attention. He turned as a sleek, furry body slid on its back down the muddy trail and splashed into the water. Wonder realized the other two animals had careened down the muddy slide and knocked him into the water—though whether it had been an accident was another matter.

Three sets of eyes studied him. The third and largest creature raised its head clear of the water and began to chatter. Wonder could not understand its speech.

Regardless, the goat spoke politely. "Hello, friends. My name is Wonder."

The creatures squealed and chattered and gestured, but the unintelligible barrage was interrupted by the gravelly voice of the crow. "CRAACK! Wet goat," he said ruefully, shaking his head.

Wonder turned toward Mac Craack, "Master Crow, what are they?"

"GRAAWK. Large one Jessie. Little ones kit one and kit two. No names yet. Jimbob nearby."

The creatures jabbered gaily at the crow, waving their small, furry paws as if inviting him into the stream for a swim.

"Welcome Otter Water. Meet otters," interpreted the crow.

Otter chatter again filled the air. Wonder grew very quiet, settling into his feelings. A winsome smile came to his face, and he laughed. "Mac Craack, these are the creatures I was warned about. But they're not dangerous. "Waters of the Others" was wrong. It's Otter Water!"

M.C. chuckled. "Wise goat returns. GAW, GAW, GAW. Dreams flawed, nay?"

The goat looked at the crow sharply. "Do you mean my dream about Oren was wrong?"

The crow did not answer but looked at Wonder intently. "Feel," he said.

Wonder blocked out the sound of cavorting otters and drew within himself. He quieted, listened, and felt.

A moment later, the young goat sighed. "Oren is fine. I don't know how I know it, but so it is."

With a nod, Mac Craack said simply, "Wise goat."

14

LYDIA

WITH MAC CRAACK TRANSLATING, THE TWO YOUNG OTTERS invited Wonder to play. The crow had more reconnaissance to do and was content to allow Wonder a day of rest, which the goat gladly accepted.

Before Mac Craack departed, Wonder asked, "Master Crow, why can't I understand them?"

"No words needed. Play speaks louder." And with that the crow cackled, launched into the air, and quickly flew away.

Wonder returned his attention to the otters just as one of the kits splashed him, chattered, and then ducked away into the water. Wonder hesitated for a moment and then jumped into the stream. Over the next few hours, the kits entertained him with their grace and endless frolicking. A non-stop stream of banter accompanied their antics, and though Wonder wished he knew exactly what they were saying, he got the gist of it. Play did indeed speak louder than words.

Periodically, Jessie would swim over to check on her kits. Sometimes, a large russet-furred otter accompanied her; Wonder decided that must be Jimbob. They seemed utterly unconcerned about the goat in their midst. Wonder noted that a sense of confidence and security radiated from the two older otters.

Before long, he noticed that he understood a great deal about the two kits simply through their actions. The female was slightly larger and a shade lighter in color, with reddish highlights in her coat. The male displayed some reticence, perhaps even shyness, while his sister was entirely engaged . . . and engaging.

Water being a less than ideal element for Wonder, he soon retired to the bank and settled into a dense mat of bunch grass. He was happy to watch the kits swim and play on the muddy bank while the sun dried his coat. Every now and again, the female kit would leap over or feint and dash around him, chattering all the while.

After grazing a bit, Wonder dozed in the sun, untroubled by dark dreams. But his gentle slumber ended with a start when a mollusk shell caromed off his nose. The air filled with otter giggles as the two kits roiled the water very close to him. He instantly knew that they had tossed the shell at him.

Wonder cracked open one eye, saw the grinning faces of his new friends waiting expectantly for him to play, and then bounded toward them in one great leap. The otters were so quick Wonder knew they would slip away while he was still in midair. They squeaked and jumped back, leaving Wonder to dance a mad jig in the shallows as the kits splashed about gaily.

After a few minutes, Wonder relaxed in the shallows and settled comfortably into the moment and an inner quiet. The female kit's head emerged from the water inches from his nose. Her eyes gazed intently at him, deep brown and twinkling, as a silent communion took hold of them. Something indescribable passed between them, and adoration filled the goat. He saw a shiver pass through her, and knew intuitively that she had felt the same.

A name for her came to him. As he whispered it into the vibrant space between them, he knew it fit her. "Lydia."

The light grew in the otter's eyes, and she repeated it. "Lydia." Then, in words he could clearly understand for the first time since meeting the otter family, she said, "Hi, Wonder. My name is Lydia."

Then she splashed him and dove into the pool.

Wonder backed onto the bank and settled again into the grass. Quieting, he felt and listened. Long moments passed before words bubbled up from the stillness. So faint he almost thought he imagined it, a voice spoke. "Relating is recognizing only One, no other."

Wonder blinked several times in rapid succession as he considered the words. An extraordinary feeling of contentment welled up in his chest.

It was only when he heard Mac Craack announce, "Goat gone. Only Wonder" that the goat returned from his reverie.

He looked at Mac Craack and began to speak, "Master Crow . . . ."

But the crow cut him off. "GRAWWK! Speak not. Keep within. Now!"

And Wonder spoke not.

The crow peered at him for a moment before continuing. "Oren good. Says, 'What is is. What we think is not. Touch it. Taste it. Smell it. Think it. It is not it. It is beyond sense. Non-sense.' "

Wonder tried to speak and was cut off again by the crow. So he quieted and drew within.

Mac Craack sat on his branch and watched Wonder as the day faded. Then the crow silently led him back to the undergrowth in the lee of the overhang.

Wonder rested long in contemplation. Mac Craack had flown all the way back to the farm just to reassure him, but even before the crow returned, Wonder had sensed that Oren was all right. Wonder had spent the day making new friends, creatures who accepted him without question or ridicule, and had even forged a deep connection with Lydia that he didn't fully understand.

And then there was the voice inside, the Presence that spoke wisdom to Wonder, if only he could be quiet and still enough to hear it. The Presence knew things Wonder did not. How was that even possible, if the voice came from inside him?

Wonder pondered these things and more as he lay awake, listening to the lullaby of running water. Just before sleep fell upon him, Oren's message, garbled though it was by Mac Craack's peculiar way of speaking, made sense: touching or tasting or smelling something, or even thinking of it or feeling it, was only one facet of knowing. When he had looked into Lydia's eyes, he had known her not as an otter or anything that he could describe with his limited senses but in the deep, quiet way he sometimes knew things when he listened to the inner voice.

As Wonder drifted off, his sleepy mind was filled with otter giggles and twinkling brown eyes.

15

Danger in the Grass

The next morning, Wonder crept from his cover. On the other side of the stream stood a small herd of deer. Several tentatively bent to drink while the lead buck slowly scanned their surroundings. His vision locked in on Wonder. He snorted and lowered his head slightly, showing Wonder the points of his antlers. Soundlessly, a ripple of concern passed to the other deer as they shifted to alert readiness.

After a moment, the buck determined that Wonder was no danger, and a sense of vigilant ease settled back into the herd. Wonder stepped forward as Mac Craack glided in on the morning breeze.

"Wild goat . . . GAW, GAW, GAW!" the crow laughed.

"Good morning, Master Crow," said Wonder.

"Eat. Drink. Mac Craack is right back," he announced as he flew westward.

Wonder approached the stream just as the deer finished and walked gracefully away. The morning was still but filled with the calls of birds. Wonder grazed on grasses and also on some delicious new shoots he found on a stand of brush.

A short time later, all four otters poked their wet muzzles from the water. They jabbered away endlessly as the goat lay down in a patch of grass and listened. He couldn't understand them today, but he hadn't really expected to. Lydia crept from the water just as Mac Craack returned and roosted on a lower branch. She picked her way gracefully toward Wonder and then touched her tiny nose to his for a moment. She skittered to the side to lock her gaze boldly into one of his eyes. Long moments passed before she returned to the water with her family and the otter chatter resumed.

Mac Craack spoke. "Wonder full. Otter full. Perfect goodbye. Touch and go. Ay?"

Wonder asked wistfully, "We must go then?"

The crow nodded. "Leave valley. Over hill. Drink up. Little water." Then Mac Craack burst upward in a swirl of black feathers and flew ahead.

Wonder drank long. Then he looked to the otters. Jimbob and kit one had disappeared, but Jessie and Lydia were watching him. He nodded to them, and Lydia chattered delightedly. Wonder did not say goodbye—they wouldn't have understood him anyway—as he turned and trotted away from the stream toward a notch in the bluffs.

Soon afterward, the country opened up into rolling grassland. For the next several hours, he moved steadily higher. Occasionally, Mac Craack would swoop by and monitor his progress. Around midday, Wonder reached the crest of the rising land. Beyond it was a valley running north to south. Another stream glinted in the sunlight as it traced its way through the land. The lush green grass shimmered as a light breeze tickled the landscape. Beyond the valley, foothills rose into the mountains, which now looked much closer than they had before. The distance was another illusion, Wonder realized—one more reason to question what he perceived.

Mac Craack alit on the ground beside Wonder. "GRAACK! Eat now. Rest. Water ahead."

Wonder alternated between grazing and scanning the vista. He noted contours in the mountains now, purple giving way to green. To the south he watched pronghorn move ghostlike over the folds of land. Wildflowers dotted the terrain, and he could taste their sweetness on the breeze.

After a short rest, the crow prodded the goat forward, and they began a steady descent toward the next valley. Some time later, Mac

Craack led him to a tiny spring burbling from the ground. Wonder was quite thirsty, and the water was very sweet. He drank his fill before they resumed their trek.

Soon, Wonder noticed an approaching drop in the land. They arrived at bluffs steep enough that Mac Craack had to lead the goat through a narrow passage Wonder would never have found on his own. Just before exiting into the lower grasslands, the crow soared away to search ahead. With the bluffs behind him, Wonder paused for a moment to watch Mac Craack soar on the thermal updrafts.

A movement to his left drew his attention. When he saw what lurked there, he held his breath as he unconsciously backed toward the bluff. Two coyotes had emerged from deep grasses. Red tongues lolling, eyes darting, they watched Wonder with great interest . . . and hunger.

16

Coy Dogs

WONDER PRESSED AGAINST THE WARM STONE OF THE BLUFF. He felt a twinge of fear as the two coyotes split up. His gaze darted between them, trying to track both at once. The larger moved stealthily in a curved path to bring it slightly to Wonder's side, while the other moved in a crouch toward the bluff to attack the goat's flank. All the while, the coyotes' stares never wavered, focusing intently on their prey.

The young goat quivered with fear, but he realized that the fear did him no good, so he named it, as Oren had taught him, and put it aside. He made himself go quiet and still, inhabiting the moment. Absolute clarity came to him, and he realized what he needed to do. He turned his head to fearlessly stare at the coyote at his flank and then looked back to the one at his fore.

He spoke with conviction. "My name is Wonder. But I am not that."

The coyotes glanced at each other, puzzled. And then Wonder charged. The coyote in front of him tilted its head in surprise, never expecting its prey to act so aggressively. It didn't move even as the goat's rapid strides carried him toward a collision. Wonder lowered his head to butt his foe.

Then just before Wonder crashed into the coyote, a black form dropped like a stone from the sky. A fierce cry echoed, "GRAAWK!"

The coyote leaped sideways to dodge the assault from above.

Wonder slammed into it at full force, striking a few inches behind its shoulder. The snap of ribs cracking was immediately followed by a pained yelp as the coyote tumbled to the ground.

Wonder whirled to face the second coyote. Its yellow eyes flitted between the goat and the crow above, seemingly unsure which was the bigger threat. Wonder quickly repositioned himself so he could face the smaller coyote while still watching the first as it dragged itself to its feet.

Wonder prepared for another charge, but Mac Craack got there first. A ferocious cry came from above, and again the black form flashed through the air. The second coyote was prepared and tried to snap at the crow. Yet Mac Craack, moving at a seemingly impossible speed, altered his course and scraped his claws across the coyote's eyes. He wheeled away, cackling insults, as a few black feathers floated to the ground. The coyote slung itself low to the ground and whimpered.

Wonder spoke with determination. "My name is Wonder. But I am not that. And I am not afraid."

The coyotes began a slinking, limping retreat, glancing furtively from the sky to the goat as they crept away.

"CRAWCK! Run coy dogs!" Mac Craack swept low over Wonder and said, "Quick. Go. Now."

The goat galloped away, following the crow's path overhead. As he escaped the narrow passage, he heard a mournful, bitter howl. Glancing over his shoulder, he saw the yellow eyes of the disappointed coyotes watching their dinner escape. Wonder raced down the gentle slope. Soon the sounds of stones buried beneath the soil thudded against his hooves, signaling his arrival in the valley.

Mac Craack flew over a small stand of trees, and Wonder rushed through them to the side of the stream. The crow urged him into the current and slightly upstream to a small islet covered with a dense thicket. He threaded his way into the center of the thicket, where a small trickle ran. It was an excellent and well-protected place for Wonder to halt.

As he bent to quench his thirst, Mac Craack alit on a branch of a sturdy cottonwood to survey their surroundings. After drinking his fill, Wonder lay in the water to cool off.

Well, he thought, *it didn't kill me, so I guess I must be stronger.*

17

THE RETURN OF
FOOL'S GOAT

JUST BEFORE DUSK, MAC CRAACK DESCENDED TO PERCH ON branches above Wonder's head. "Coy dogs not dogging us. Fearful dogs fear goat. GAW! And mighty Master Crow! GAW! GAW! GAW!"

The goat laughed easily along with the crow. The mad dash had burned off all his energy, and he'd been lying quietly for some time, thinking about the attack.

"Master Crow, I'm afraid I am 'Fool's Goat,' as old Manuel said. What goat, other than a foolish one, would attack coyotes?"

The crow cocked his head and shrugged his wings. Then he blinked, and Wonder realized that the crow was regarding him with not one but two bright black eyes.

"M.C., what happened to your eye?"

The crow winked first one eye and then the other. "Eye . . . eye . . . eye . . . eye," he chanted with obnoxious pleasure.

"Mac Craack, you have your eye back! How can that be?"

"Wise goat gone. CRAACK!" The crow shook his head. "What is is. What we think is not."

Wonder frowned. "But I distinctly remember that you only had one eye before today!"

"NOW! Listen. Feel. Quiet."

And the goat drew within himself to consider this strange development. He breathed deeply. No answer came, but his questions vanished.

"Okay, M.C. What is is."

Mac Craack jumped down to a lower branch and tapped his beak gently right between Wonder's eyes. "See not with eyes. See with heart." He pecked the goat hard on the nose. "See?"

Wonder could not help but laugh even as he scrubbed a foreleg across his smarting nose. "Yes, Master Crow, I understand. I'm just not accustomed to missing eyes being found."

"GAW, GAW!" laughed the crow. "Trust not appearance. No eye. Now eye." He paused. "Hungry goat?"

Knowing that the mystery of the lost-and-now-found eye would not soon be solved—at least not with Mac Craack's help—Wonder nodded. He forded the stream to reach a dense patch of mixed grass and forbs on the other side. There were even some small shrubs Wonder had never before seen that tasted better than anything he'd yet known. As he browsed happily, the crow found a comfortable spot on a branch and watched him.

"Fool's Goat, ay?" he asked.

Wonder shrugged and pulled up another mouthful of grass. "Fool's Goat. No goat. I don't know."

Mac Craack chuckled. "Pain gone?"

"No eye. Now eye. Now pain. No pain. I guess the hurt is gone. At least for this moment." Wonder searched his feelings. It seemed that the shame tied to the formerly ugly name was indeed gone.

The moon, huge and orange, began to slide above the horizon. Exhausted, Wonder slipped into a fearless, dreamless sleep, sprawled on the grass beneath the overarching trees.

18

FOOTHILLS

A DULL THUD STARTLED THE GOAT AWAKE SHORTLY AFTER dawn. It took a second thump, this one on the back of his neck, to cause him to look upward. Two squirrels, both a deep brown that was almost black, barked at him as another nut dropped, narrowly missing his nose. When they saw Wonder looking at them, they snickered and darted farther up the trunk of the tree.

Wonder arose and shook himself, leaving the squirrels to their antics. He felt refreshed by his long sleep, and was surprised that he'd managed to slumber so soundly out in the open. Rather than hiding in caves or brambles, Wonder had simply fallen asleep at the stream's edge. Out of an inner quiet that seemed to magnify the outer solitude, a thought came to him: *I'm safe, no matter what. I proved that to myself on this journey.*

Mac Craack was already aloft, so Wonder ambled over to the stream for a drink and then began a leisurely breakfast graze. Other than the sounds of moving water and the occasional barking of squirrels, it was quite peaceful.

An instant later, Mac Craack announced his arrival with a great call and a thrashing of wings, shattering the early morning quiet.

"Faith-full goat?"

Wonder looked interestedly at the crow. "I was just thinking something like that, M.C. How did you know that?"

"Where is knowing?" countered Mac Craack.

After a moment to consider the question, Wonder chuckled and said, "I see."

"Master Goat soon!" croaked the crow. "Heart sees, heart knows."

Wonder nodded solemnly. "I knew that. And now I know that trust is not what I've been taught, M.C. Gullibility is not faith; it's foolishness. Our trek has shown me that I can rest in assurance, and so I rest assured. It is not imagined. It is based on my experiences. Experience teaches me I can trust the path. And trust myself as well."

"GRAWK!" erupted from Mac Craack followed by the crow's gravelly chortle. "Not even to mountain yet. Wonder is a wonder!"

The crow launched into the air again and flew toward the foothills. Wonder bent to take a few mouthfuls of water and then resumed grazing. After a little while, he settled comfortably into the grass. For an hour or more, he simply watched and listened, both outwardly and inwardly, until Mac Craack returned.

"Foothills tricky. Canyons trickier. Follow good deer trail. Deer goat, ay?"

Wonder rose, now well rested and energized. "Lead on, Master Crow," he said confidently, and fell into an easy trot as Mac Craack flew westward.

The land began a steady, gradual ascent. Grasses thinned as spiny shrubs cluttered sloping ground. A few cacti sprouted along the edge of the narrow track as the soil gave way to rocky scree. As the terrain rose, so did the temperature, the heat radiating from rock already warmed by the morning sun.

Wonder followed a rough trail that meandered ever higher and farther westward. The heat, rock, and scrub made for a wearying climb. Little more than lizards and jackrabbits showed themselves, though occasional screeches of scrub jays pierced the air. Wonder kept a steady eye on Mac Craack, who zigzagged and tumbled through the air a little ways ahead. Above, flying much higher than the crow, hawks soared on rising thermals.

The goat grew thirsty as he plodded through the harsh land, but the drainages were completely dry. After some time, the crow flew down to perch on an ancient and gnarled juniper bush.

"Tired goat? Or is goat just tired?" he squawked.

"What is that supposed to mean?" Wonder asked, a touch of annoyance in his voice. He swallowed his frustrations and mustered the deference due to an elder. "Master Crow, if there is a point in your question, I'll need some clarification."

Mac Craack cocked his head. "Pity goat, nay?" he asked. "GRAWK. Is tiredness you?"

Wonder shook his head slowly. "Of course not, M.C. But this goat's body is tiring."

"Water round bend," announced the crow as he scrutinized Wonder with many angled cants of his head. "Rest too!"

Wonder nodded and plodded forward. Everything was dry and dusty, and he could not see any trees to indicate running water. Still, his gait quickened in anticipation of a drink. Clambering up a rise, Wonder looked out to see a wide, flat expanse pockmarked with a great many small mounds. A prairie dog sentinel barked an alarm, followed by a great scurrying among her fellows. Tiny figures stood poised over their holes, heads turned toward him.

To the right, beneath a curving wall of packed and layered sediment, ran a sandy wash. There was no sign of water, but the grasses and scrub along it were tinged with green.

Wonder saw Mac Craack settle onto a branch of a shrub dangling over the earthen embankment. Slowly descending the deer trail, the goat continued to scan the prairie dog colony as the small creatures resumed their normal comings and goings. Drawing into the shade of the overhang, Wonder looked up at the crow, who motioned with a downward dip of his beak.

"Dig," M.C. announced.

Wonder looked at the crow skeptically, but he began to dig. Steady movements of his weary forelegs produced a small trench. Soon water began to seep into it. Though brownish with silt, the water refreshed him. He was quite thirsty and quickly drained the trench, but he found that if he waited, it would fill again. Then he began to browse, moving into the sun for a few choice mouthfuls before retreating back to the shade.

After his meager meal, Wonder collapsed on the dusty ground and fell asleep.

19

SIGNS AND WONDERS

SHADOWS WERE LONG UPON THE GROUND WHEN WONDER woke from dozing, lethargic with sleep. Mac Craack was nowhere in sight. Nearby, the prairie dogs barked and chased each other around and around their village. He watched them, mesmerized, as a quiet grew within him. It was much like the peaceful silence he remembered so well from his time with Oren, but deeper and somehow more quiet.

He could feel breath slowly moving through him. His gaze softened; the prairie dogs' appearance began to shift, as did the backdrop of plants and earth, becoming less distinct. Even as his vision blurred, realness grew.

A still, small voice arose out of nothingness. "Breathe," it said softly. In response, Wonder breathed attentively. Time stood still.

"Do you know how to breathe?" the voice whispered.

Even as it spoke, Wonder knew there was no answer.

"Or are you breathed? Be still and feel," the voice said. "Feel and know in absence there is Presence . . . . Feel now."

And feeling filled him. It was as if Presence had summoned it and then responded to Itself, a chanting call and response, all from beyond the goat.

Time passed, though Wonder did not know it until the voice again spoke. "All the time in the world. All there is is now." After a long pause, it trailed away almost musically with a cadence of "Breathe . . . now . . . breathe . . . now . . . breathe . . ."

Wonder remained motionless even as he returned from that distant place. Then his eyes, moving almost imperceptibly, scanned the open expanse before him. It was dusk. The scene shimmered. Subtle differences in the wavering atmosphere differentiated earth from grasses and shrubs and still further from sky. More distinctive were the vibrations of prairie dogs moving furtively in the shadows.

A sentinel barked, and somehow Wonder recognized the kinship between squirrels and prairie dogs. The sound was more than just communication; it bound the colony of prairie dogs together as a single being. As he gazed farther into the shimmering twilight world, that sense of interrelatedness grew. The waves that seemed to lie behind the forms were not separate or distinct but woven together like a mat of tangled roots.

He turned his attention from the creatures, and found that rock was only slightly removed from brush or air. Wonder noted the striations of earth across the embankment. Time revealed itself as gravel gave way to sand, which gave way to silt. Throughout the layers were stray pebbles, petrified organic matter, bits of bone, and other artifacts. Wonder saw it all as a process, a constantly unfolding soup of apparently separate objects. But all were related, connected by ever moving, throbbing waves of pure energy.

A bolt of lightning struck in the distance and jolted him into a more physically present awareness. Wonder lifted himself from the ground and shook his body. He knew Mac Craack watched from above even before he looked up.

"CRAACK," announced the crow. "Welcome back, goat of wonder!" His tone gave away his amusement, but it was infused with fondness as well.

"I never left," said Wonder. "But I feel as though I've been elsewhere."

"Signs and wonders. Or is Wonder a sign?" M.C. shrugged. "Matters not."

In the light of the setting sun, Wonder saw that Mac Craack's formerly ragged and windswept plumage looked sleeker and glossier. His black feathers were tinged with rainbows now.

"See!" pronounced M.C. "GAW, GAW, GAW!"

The goat nodded slowly. There was no question to be asked in return.

"Now, Craacked Goat?"

Again, Wonder nodded before speaking with great care. "Master Crow, it's all Presence, regardless of appearance."

A long, quiet moment passed. Coyotes wailed in the distance, singing their lament to the rising moon. A perfumed scent of rain swept across the dry earth, and an instant later, fat drops of water began to fall, cratering the powdery soil.

Mac Craack turned and looked over his shoulder. "Lovely goat soon to be tumble goat. Water comes."

Wonder glanced up the wash. He saw the initial trickle of what would soon be a tumultuous flood cascading down the mountain. He knew that too as yet one more aspect of perfection even as he moved away toward safer terrain.

20

RED ROCK

MORNING SPRANG FORTH CLEAN AND CRISP, THE LAND REfreshed by the storm. Wonder had slept in the lee of a boulder above the wash, and when he awoke, he found Mac Craack perched on the rock directly in front of him.

"Good morning, Master Crow," he said, getting to his feet and stretching. "What does the day hold forth?"

"CRAACK," said the bird. "Steep climb. New sights. New eyes." With a joyful cry, he leaped into the air.

Wonder considered the crow thoughtfully. "M.C., how is it that you're always so optimistic? Is there nothing that troubles you?"

Mac Craack landed again and scratched his underbelly with one clawed foot. Then he shook a wing. Next came a guttural cough.

The crow peered at the goat. "See, inquisitive goat?"

Wonder began to speak, but M.C. stopped him with an earsplitting "LISTEN!" followed promptly by an equally loud "SEE!"

Wonder did as he was told. After the shimmering insight of the evening before, he half expected to sense the answers right away. Presence, however, did not choose to grace Wonder that morning. After a lengthy pause, he announced, "I'll have to hold my thoughts until I have more clarity."

"CAW," chuckled Mac Craack. "Slow goat? Or does goat go slow?"

Wonder snorted. "Perhaps I should keep my own counsel until I'm sure what needs to be said or done." He watched to see the crow's response.

M.C. laughed loudly. "Blunder Goat!" His amused caws continued as he leaped into the sky and swept away. "Come, Blunder!"

Bewildered, the goat rose and ambled down into the wash. Finding a trickle of water still running, Wonder drank his fill, snatched a few bites of grass, and began a steady trot up the drainage.

Before long, the trail steepened as it wove crazily through rock-strewn terrain. Juniper and mountain mahogany began to replace the brush. Soon piñon trees appeared, and the trail grew even more challenging.

Wonder found himself having to jump over and onto boulders. The sun rose in the sky and began to bake the rocks. As the day grew hotter and the climb more arduous, Wonder's limbs began to feel the strain. It seemed like Mac Craack was deliberately testing him by setting a punishing pace and offering little guidance. Every now and again, he would appear above boulders and call out, but more often than not, Wonder found himself having to renegotiate his way when he found it impassable.

As his weariness grew and the climb lengthened, he slipped more often. One particularly bad section resulted in several bruising falls. After crashing into a heap yet again, Wonder mumbled, "My name is Wonder, and I will not be deterred." He picked himself up one more time and pressed on. Whenever it appeared that flatter ground was at hand, another turn would reveal more of the difficult terrain.

Finally, well into the afternoon and after a long day without water, he crested a rocky ridge and beheld a vista that made him forget his exhaustion. A red rock rampart angled across the mountain, giving way to a canyon heading directly to the west. Never before had he seen rock so rich in color. Above the canyon was a forest of massive ponderosa pines. Beyond that, Wonder saw a sweep of brilliant green vegetation that appeared to alternate between meadows and smaller trees stunted by the elevation. Still higher were craggy rock walls of granite that gave way to upward-sloping snowfields, brilliant white beneath turquoise skies.

He heard the crow settle near him with a flapping of wings, but he dared not look away from the scene. Finally, drunk on the beauty and majesty of the landscape, he turned toward M.C. Nodding appreciatively, he said, "It was a hard climb, but this view makes it all worthwhile."

Mac Craack's black eyes studied him for a moment, and then he cackled, "Blundering along! GAW! GAW! GAW!"

Wonder blinked in silent contemplation. "Presence gives us moments, and for those moments, we live."

"Wonder blunders, wisdom appears!" M.C. paused and turned to gaze up at the peak before them, then danced into the air. "CRAACK! Come, blunder! Wonder awaits!"

The bird flew toward the canyon. Wonder followed slowly, for even in the few moments of rest, his limbs had stiffened. The two travelers crossed the escarpment, and Wonder paused to marvel at the rich color of the red rock. He had never seen anything like it.

The trail wound up the canyon. It glowed in the late afternoon light, the red rock emanating heat and energy. But after a time, Wonder again took note of his weary body and a thirst that had become overpowering. As the way narrowed and the sun began to sink, shadows eased the heat but did nothing for his thirst.

Then, unexpectedly, the canyon came to an abrupt end. Wonder could see no way to advance, and M.C. was nowhere in sight. The goat studied the rock walls for a long time. Still no path, and still no crow.

As he turned in hopes of finding a solution, a wrenching pain shot through his right hindquarter as a muscle that had been overworked and deprived of water for too long seized. Wonder collapsed with a screeching bleat. The white-hot agony blinded him to everything as he writhed in the sand.

21

Boboso

Slowly, Wonder quieted himself. The pain remained intense, but when he extended his leg, there was some relief. He lay on his side, breathing shallowly, and waited for the crow to swoop down and save him once more. As dusk approached, he risked calling out for Mac Craack. When no response came, a kernel of fear grew in him.

Taking a deep breath, he reached deeper inside himself, deeper into the quiet that lay like a placid lake beyond the pain and the fear. *My name is Wonder, but I am not that. This will not kill me. It will make me stronger.* His resolve grew in response, but the cramp remained. He concentrated more deeply, pulling from a well he did not know existed. *My name is Wonder, but I am not that.*

Then a surprising thought bubbled up from the well: *I may very well die from this, or some other misstep on my trek.*

Realization shot through him—his understanding of his father's mantra was wrong. Wonder was mortal, and even if a hundred scrapes and adventures made him stronger, the hundred-first might kill him. Rather than being disconcerting, the thought brought forth deeper insight. *My name is Wonder, but I am not that. Even if the goat dies, I do not. Presence lives as me. Not I! Not I! Not I!*

The fear vanished. More peace than he had ever known settled over him. With it, the muscle spasm began to ease. Still, Wonder was exhausted, and night was rapidly approaching. He was able to roll onto his belly, but his hindquarter still ached. And he was terribly thirsty.

He heard a snuffling sound then. As if by magic, a large black bear had appeared from the box end of the canyon. He was sniffing the air, catching Wonder's scent.

Fearlessly Wonder announced, "My name is Wonder, but I am not that. And I am not afraid."

The bear's head swung toward the voice, pinpointing with scent and sound what vision could not. He spoke in a childlike, sing-song voice, and Wonder thought the bear must not be very bright. "Wonder, wonder who?" The bear's head swung as if choreographed to the words. "Wonder who smells like goat?"

"Some would call me a goat, but I am not that," Wonder replied.

The bear snuffled some more. "Hmm . . . if not a goat, goat, and not Wonder, Wonder, then what might you be?"

A flash of remembrance shot through Wonder. He recalled when Mac Craack had first appeared, and Oren had underestimated him. Intuition told him there was more to this bear than he imagined.

"So Master Bear, do you have a name I might use to properly address you?"

"Master Bear, hmm, Master Goat? My name is Boboso, and I am that, except when I choose not to be, or when riddling with a goat that is not a goat."

Wonder laughed with delight. "You are very wise, Master Bear."

Boboso harrumphed. "Hardly wise but always a student, Master Goat." The bear raised his nose as if to catch some odor before resuming. "Where do you think you are, Wonder who is not Wonder? And where are you bound?"

"I'm going to the top of the mountain."

"I see," said Boboso. "Where are you now?"

"I seem to be at the end of a box canyon, and my guide, Mac Craack Crow, is missing. I do not know the way."

The bear bobbed his head as he considered this. "Be assured, Mac Craack Crow is not lost. No crow ever is. And neither are you."

"But there is no path, Boboso."

"No goat that was not a wonder would blunder here. Certainly, you are on the path."

"Blunder, Master Bear? That is the word Mac Craack used several times today."

A toothy smile came to the bear's face. "Serendipity strikes, Wonder. The eldest of the bear clan, Anthony the Mellow, says, 'The path is every step. Lift your vision above the muck.' And, I would add, blunder is not possible. No way, no how."

Wonder struggled to his feet, wincing as his stiff limbs stretched. "Then I will keep my eyes on the mountaintop with every step I take."

Boboso simply nodded his head.

"Master Bear, Boboso, I have always heard a goat should fear a bear. Would I not make a fine meal for you and your kin?"

He harrumphed again. "Anthony the Mellow says, 'With sight on high, there can be no harm.' "

The bear again raised his snout to the air, sniffed, and turned, noticing some other scent on the breeze. "Go now, Wonder not Wonder."

"Thank you, Master Bear. I will not forget you."

Wonder walked straight at the canyon wall, but he kept his gaze angled upward at the mountain. A nearly full moon had risen, and it cast a pale light over the canyon. Stepping onto a low shoulder of rock, still looking up, he spied a small, recessed ledge. Despite a dull ache still remaining from his muscle spasms, a quick jump brought him safely up onto the ledge. Now he could see a crease above him in the rock that had been invisible from below. With eyes cast upward, Wonder climbed, and in just a few moments, the crease widened to reveal a narrow cleft.

Up ahead, he saw a pool of rainwater with hardscrabble and bunch grasses surrounding it. Before lowering his head to drink and eat, he lifted his sight once more to the moonlit peak and whispered his thanks.

22

PONDEROSA PINES

"G RAWWK!"
Wonder awoke with a start and leaped to his feet, sending
up a swirling cloud of dry country dust from his makeshift bed.
Aching muscles protested, but he bounded forward to greet Mac
Craack. In the goat's estimation, the crow was larger and glossier
than he remembered him, but he did not mention it.

"Good morning, Master Crow, not lost but now found."

Mac Craack blinked a few times as a whimsical look passed
across his usually inscrutable face. "Goat never lost, nay?"

Wonder bleated softly with affection. "No, M.C. No way. No how."

"Good Goat! Eat now. Stroll today." The crow leaped from a
ledge and flew away. Wonder shook the remaining dust from his
coat and walked stiffly to the pool of water. Between sips, he studied the slope above that led into the ponderosa forest. He saw that
the hillside drained into the cleft where he stood, which then cascaded down into the canyon below. It would be a beautiful waterfall
during a storm, and its remnant was this pool of clear, cold water.

The sparkling of the sunlight on the water made Wonder think
of twinkling otter eyes, and he suddenly remembered that Lydia
had come to him in his dreams during the depths of his past night's
slumber. He was sure it was her, though her form was not so clear.
He paused and gazed up toward the forest in curious contemplation. Knowing she was somehow inexplicably with him caused an
intense feeling of joy inside Wonder. He puzzled over it for a time.

Then he concluded he did not know what to make of it, and returned to browsing.

A short while later, he was clambering over the last of the rocks. Before him rose the tall pines. In their shade, it was quiet and cool. A deer trail wound through the giant trunks, and Wonder followed this path at a slow and easy pace. There was a gentleness among the ponderosas. Layers of pine needles, soft beneath Wonder's aching hooves, muffled all sound.

For a few hours, he ambled along as the trail climbed slightly. At regular intervals, squirrels hectored him for intruding into their domain, but otherwise, it was a peaceful morning walk. Sometime around midday, Wonder emerged from the dim canopy of pines into brilliant sunshine. Before him was a large meadow in which stood a number of very large, deer-like creatures. With their spreading antlers, the towering males were like walking trees.

Wonder studied them and then noticed Mac Craack awaiting him on a small sapling. He strolled over. "Good day, M.C. I seem to have found you, as well as animals I do not know."

"Elk, ay" said the crow.

Wonder watched the animals for a few moments before replying, "I thought elk were animals of the plains."

"Prairies once. Like bison. Now only here."

Wonder nodded thoughtfully. "Things are never as they seem, are they M.C.? We don't know that we don't know."

"CRAACK," came the response. "Questions make goat wise."

Together, they watched the elk for some time before Mac Craack took to the air once more. Wonder was captivated by the graceful movements of the large creatures. Eventually he trotted around the elk, keeping to the fringe of the meadow as he circled toward the west and the rock walls. They raised their heads to watch him as he passed, seemingly as mystified by the appearance of a small white goat as he had been by theirs.

Soon the land sloped upward again. Grasses were replaced by a forest of stunted oak trees no taller than Wonder. Trails dotted with bunch grasses and wildflowers meandered throughout the small trees like a maze. It remained easy going as the afternoon passed, accompanied by the sounds of gentle mountain breezes, birds, and the buzzing of insects. With the variety of plants, it was likewise easy to grab bites to eat along the way.

Eventually even the scrubby oaks fell away, replaced by scattered alpine brush and rock. His trail and others slowly converged into a single well-worn path that skirted the now-upswelling granite. Mac Craack stayed close, flying from perch to perch as Wonder moved steadily forward and upward.

Though he was beginning to tire, Wonder was spurred on by the sound of rumbling water. As the day waned, the noise grew until finally he spied a small waterfall cascading in stages down from the snowfields high above the cliffs. Wonder approached a good-sized pool at the base of the falls. With tender alpine grasses and lichen spreading around the translucent blue, there was ample water and browse.

After dinner, he and Mac Craack chatted as the moon rose high above them. The conversation reminded him of his easy rapport with Oren. His lessons with the old buck seemed a very long time ago. Wonder smiled fondly at the memory. He realized with slight surprise that the fond feelings extended to all those he had encountered, even crotchety old Manuel.

"Wind rising, goat settling," said M.C.

"I feel at peace, Master Crow." Wonder quietly observed his surroundings, letting his senses drink in the sights, sounds, and smells. After a lengthy pause, he said, "Do you see how the wind swirls the waters? There must be a downdraft from the falls dancing with the winds sweeping up from below."

23

DANCING DREAMS

AFTER A MORNING GRAZE, WONDER DREW A FINAL DRINK OF the cold mountain water. He turned his gaze upward toward the soaring cliffs and spotted Mac Craack high above. With a quick and invigorating shake from head to hoof, he took the first step of the day's trek.

Today, the path was quite steep. And dangerous too, Wonder thought, not from the footing, which was good as long as he remained securely on the path, but from the quickly increasing height from which he might fall with a single misstep.

Absorbed into the present by each step, Wonder soon fell into a mesmerized state. Concentrating carefully on what lay immediately in front of him, the goat soon lost all track of time and distance. Not once did Mac Craack come to point him on his way. It was as if the path had come to reside within him, yet if he had been asked what came beyond the immediate step, he would have been unable to say.

So it was with some surprise that after an inward curving loop into a deeply shadowed crease in the face of the cliff, a glossy orange rock dropped right in front of his upraised hoof just as it crossed into sunlight from shadow. His hoof hovered as the glint of the light on the stone arrested him. He studied it for a long instant before raising his head to see from where it had fallen.

Before him on the trail was a great drop-off. Beyond it, the mountains unfurled, giving way to the undulations of the foothills and the smooth, golden highland prairie beyond. The goat was amazed that he could see so much, a vast panorama.

Without knowing why, Wonder softened his gaze. He imagined that the veil of the world had parted to reveal nothing but pulsing energy. It steadily ebbed and flowed as he watched, and he felt again the shimmering interconnectedness of all things. Time stood still until something caromed off his muzzle, causing him to look upward again.

M.C. looked down from an overhanging rock with his head half cocked. Wonder puzzled that the crow's feathers now seemed mottled with gray and white, though the edges that outlined his shape were remarkably precise.

"Wonder wondering?" the crow asked.

The goat chortled. "M.C., do you know what I have seen?"

"CAWK!" he croaked, his black eyes dancing with amusement. "A crow? Wonderful sight indeed!"

"You do know, you wily old bird. And where did you get the strange orange stone?"

"CRAACK!" he announced. "Wonder!"

"What, M.C.?"

"Wonder, look!"

The goat gazed down to see that the stone was no longer there. He swiveled his head up with his mouth open in surprise.

"Made it up, Wonder the No Goat. All made up. Make believe. Believe and make."

Wonder blinked a few times as he contemplated this information. He glanced to the horizon, which now looked utterly ordinary. Softening his gaze again, the foreground of his vision grew transparent. He held the softness as he rotated his head again to look up at the crow. The waves of energy were different in the crow and still more different in the rock above him, but the veil remained parted.

"M.C., are you telling me that what we see is only an imprint over what is really there?"

Mac Craack leaned down so far that Wonder expected him to topple from his perch. He peered intently at the goat. "Story, story, story," he hissed.

Wonder breathed deeply. "It's all a story."

"CAWWK! Goat on a ledge. Go to the edge. Wisdom, Wonder, wisdom!"

With that Mac Craack launched from the rock and caught an updraft that took him aloft. Shaking his head, Wonder stepped around the corner of rock to follow the path—only to find himself face to face with a compact but powerful ram with horns curled tightly on each side of its head. The larger animal bleated softly and spoke in a sonorous voice.

"You would be Wonder, would you not?"

"That is my name, Master Ram, but it is not who I am."

The ram studied him through a lengthy silence. "You are not as large as the crow's words would have you be, though it is the size on the inside that is more the measure of a goat. Regardless, you are kin, and you are welcome." He lowered his horns and tapped his right hoof on the ground, the formal greeting between strangers of equal standing in their herd. "I am Rami of the Mountain Sheep Clan."

Rami turned adeptly on the narrow ledge, his head held high and his gait measured. Wonder followed more awkwardly as the ram sprang from the path to clamber through a boulder field. After a short distance, they came to a concealed glen nestled among the rocks. It was long and narrow with sparse grasses and a steady, trickling stream around which lounged a small herd of sheep.

Several stood and approached. Even the young ones moved with stately dignity. They welcomed him with warm formality and offered him their hospitality. When they spoke, it was not the idle chatter of the barnyard; as with their movements, there was a seriousness in their words.

After a satisfying graze, Wonder lay down by the stream and dozed in the sunshine. Neither quite asleep nor fully awake, he slipped into waking dreams. He had a vision of two bears dancing. Boboso moved nimbly beside a larger bear who was surely Anthony the Mellow. The scenes around them faded in and out. First there was the backdrop of the glen, then a red rock canyon. He even saw the familiar barnyard, which seemed smaller and more drab than he remembered it.

Then the background became a neutral gray stage on which the bears continued to dance even as they shifted shape from creature to creature. They became shaggy, big-horned sheep like Rami's clan, then mighty elk, then skittish prairie dogs, and then mischievous otters. Woven into the transitions were also inanimate objects like trees and stones. It was an odd though graceful dance, and Wonder felt a growing sense of peace as he watched it.

Back in the form of a bear, Anthony the Mellow moved without moving to peer into Wonder's face. The goat was not afraid.

Forms and settings slipped over and around him rapidly. He was the only constant, though he was neither goat nor Wonder. All the while, he felt a welling up in the place where a heart would reside. Larger and larger it grew until everything exploded into radiance. And even there he had a place, beyond form.

Boboso's voice filled the radiance, multiplied into countless rhythmic versions of his distinctive sing-song cadence. "Stories come . . . stories go . . . you and I . . . not so, not so." Over and over it went. At last, Wonder merged into the song, and all became deeply silent.

24

SUMMITING

WONDER WOKE IN THE DARKNESS AND QUIET OF EARLY morning. The sheep still slumbered around the glen, and the stream still burbled merrily, but nothing looked the same to Wonder. Today he knew himself in the way Oren had once called *bone deep*. Even if the veil never parted again, he had seen the nature of the stories that overlaid everything, and somewhere within he would not forget the truth that lay beneath the surface world.

He watched as the sun rose, bathing the sheep in golden light as they stirred from slumber. He knew that beyond that radiance was another, even brighter, light. The world was stripped before his eyes. So when Mac Craack swept in on the morning breeze, Wonder was not surprised to see an aura surrounding him.

"Master Crow, you emanate light today."

"CRAWK! Crow glows?" He preened his feathers and then spread his wings as if showing them off.

"Yes, M.C. I see. I am." He chuckled then added, "And Wonder is my name."

"Goat not goat. Ready?"

"Yes. Let me thank Rami, and we'll be on our way."

He sought out the ram, who nodded him forward with a somber point of his muzzle, and said his goodbyes. Then Wonder followed the path the crow showed from the air. He trod purposefully beneath the final, high arching rampart of rock.

Wonder glanced up to see three sturdy sheep standing like sentinels on an outcropping in the distance. To Wonder's eyes, they were a talisman, a sign of exceptional fortune. They slipped from sight as he passed through a crack in the granite walls. A few steps farther, he arrived above the rock onto a vast snowfield that stretched into the distance. Farther still he could see the graveled path curving across a ridge to the summit. He had to blink against the brightness of sun on snow. His breathing was labored in the thinning air, but the way was now easy enough.

Suddenly Mac Craack hurtled from above into a pile of soft snow. The crow swept his wings in the fine powder in what seemed to be a mad dance, all the while cackling with abandon. The snow appeared to leach the color from his feathers, but it was hard to tell with all the flying powder obscuring Mac Craack.

The goat watched until the snow settled. Had he not seen the transformation, he never would have believed that the bird who emerged was his familiar companion. Larger now and glittering white as the snow, Mac Craack performed a graceful pirouette. To Wonder's eyes, his form was without flaw.

"Blunderstruck?" croaked the familiar voice, still as rough and gravelly as ever. "GAW, GAW, GAW!"

Wonder laughed along with him, mimicking his way of speaking. "Snow crow? No crow? Master Crow!"

"GRAWK!" M.C. replied. "Funny goat! See humor, see truth, ay. GAW! GAW!"

With a stride that was now quite graceful for a creature more suited to the air, Mac Craack approached the goat. Wonder dropped his head slightly in a bow as the crow neared.

"Master Goat," M.C. croaked with authority.

Wonder steadied himself on the crusted snow, inhaled deeply, and allowed the breath to sink in. After long moments, he bowed his head lower. "Thank you."

Stock-still, they stood side by side until the crow broke the silence. "On, on, on. GRAACK!"

With that, Wonder stepped with resolve across the snowfield. He walked for hours, focused only upon each step as he took it, but eventually, he ascended the ridge and then stood atop the summit at last. M.C. dropped unerringly from the sky to a perfect perch on a crest of rock beside him. The goat slowly turned, scanning the landscape that fell away from where they stood. He saw the vista twice: first as it seemed to his eyes and then as it looked to his heart. Alternating his gaze from foreground to background to peering beyond the veil, he saw that the world was made new.

Though Wonder had reached his destination at last, he felt curiously let down. He ought to have been celebrating his achievement, but instead, he found his thoughts already turning to the next journey. He turned to the white crow and asked, "There is no end to the path, is there?"

"Only path," the crow confirmed.

Wonder considered this. At last, he said, "I see below a great river flowing south and west. I should like to see where it goes."

Part II

25

BACK AT THE BARNYARD

A BUFFER OF MYSTERY ISOLATED WONDER, OREN, AND MAC Craack from the rest of the barnyard. The other goats observed the unlikely trio with something like awe, and even the gossipy hens and Mr. and Mrs. Mule eyed them with wary respect.

When Wonder had returned on a warm, sunny afternoon, there was quite a hubbub. His surprise appearance had upset the familiar routine of barnyard life, and even as the residents gathered around to hear the tale of his trek, Wonder was aware that he had not truly returned home. The barnyard was still the same. The herd was the same. But Wonder was different, and he did not belong there anymore. Perhaps he never had. Even Maa and Paa could not overcome the distance his journey had placed between them. If any of the other goats could have given voice to it, they would have said a strangeness emanated from him, and they instinctively shied away from it.

Although the others soon lost their curiosity about Wonder, Oren and his erstwhile protégé talked at length about his adventure. As days passed and grew into seasons, every event and every nuance was carefully digested over and over again. They never tired of the inquiry it produced. For the most part, M.C. only listened when he was there, infrequently chiming in with a cackling comment.

Wonder had grown into a magnificent young buck even as Oren had aged gracefully far beyond normal years. The older buck said it was the truth that kept him vibrant and vital, but Wonder was acutely aware that his old master would not live forever. He cherished their days together even more for that.

Though Mac Craack had lost his whiteness on the return journey, the crow was still greatly improved in appearance. Iridescent black feathers flowed perfectly over his sleek and noticeably larger shape. His eye had permanently returned, and he seemed younger—or perhaps ageless.

As their ruminations continued and their understanding deepened, fewer and fewer of the events of the herd or the farm interested them. This continued until the day came when Oren asked the question that Wonder had known must come.

"Wonder, when will you leave to follow the Rio de la Vida?"

The younger goat breathed through himself before replying, "When it wants to occur."

Oren laughed. "My young friend, I know you stay only for me. That is a great kindness. But even the long life the Truth has breathed into me will soon wane. I would not have you delay on my account."

Wonder watched his mentor with a growing softness in his eyes. Moving from foreground to background and then beyond the veil, he knew his old friend's words were true.

"You are right, Master Oren. This adventure wants to commence."

"Don't fight the flow, little one. Follow it," said Oren just as Mac Craack landed at his perch. "Your guide arrives right on cue."

"CRAACK!"

They all laughed, and then Wonder asked solemnly, "Master Crow, will you accompany me on this new adventure?"

"Go crow! GAW! GAW!" he responded with his usual vigor.

26

THE LAST GOODBYE

WONDER'S DEPARTURE WAS NOT AS DIFFICULT AS THE FIRST. As he left early on a cool, comfortable day, only Oren saw him off. He had spoken with Maa and Paa the night before, and it seemed they had come to accept his need for adventure.

Wonder went so far as to give voice to it. "I cannot ignore the call of my Soul," he told them.

Nanny mirrored his thoughts perfectly. "We saw it in you from the first moments after your birth. And nothing should keep you from yourself." Then she added, "We will see you when you return."

It was challenging enough to consider he might not see Maa and Paa again, but worse was the knowledge he would not see his mentor again. The only solution was to breathe through it and experience it. With each inhalation, the ache dissolved until all that remained was a sense of pleasure. He bowed respectfully to his elder, his horns scraping the earth.

"Oren, I cannot possibly thank you enough."

The old goat chortled. "Wonder, the thanks go both ways."

The younger goat thought carefully before he responded. "So learning never ends?"

"Never," affirmed Oren.

There was a long pause during which Mac Craack launched into the air with a powerful sweep of his wings and a loud "RAWK!"

"Wonder, there is one more thing. I'm sure you already know, though you may not *know* that you know." Oren stopped and gazed across what seemed like an endless distance. Refocusing his attention on the younger goat, he spoke with great conviction. "We are all part of Oneness. You and I will see each other again because Oneness never ceases, and we are eternally bonded within it."

Wonder cocked his head with the look of curiosity he so often displayed.

Oren continued. "I have one last piece of wisdom to impart before you depart. It comes from ancient wisdom uttered by the first bird, according to Master Crow."

Wonder breathed deeply, expectantly.

"No matter what may come your way, dear one, hold this mantra closer than your heartbeat and nearer than every breath: Into the Light. Into the Light." They paused, and both Oren and Wonder lapsed into stillness. Presence descended and held them even longer. "Regardless of what seeks to distract you, hold to the Light. Even in the face of great difficulty and the hardest of questions, always into the Light."

They stood, still as stones and big as the sky, for what felt like eternity. They shared the moment as one, but all too soon, it ended.

Wonder spoke first. "Master Oren," he said, his voice full of respect and love.

The old one responded in kind. "Master Wonder."

The young buck turned and easily leaped the fence. Trotting down the slope of the pasture toward the stream, he tilted his muzzle upward, his eyes lifted to the Light.

27

THE GORGE

For many days, as Wonder worked through the initial aches and pains of muscles no longer accustomed to hard travel, the stream he and M.C. followed meandered steadily downhill away from the mountains they had gone to before. The terrain alternated between more rugged, overgrown sections and idyllic pastures. Wonder avoided confrontation with the neighboring herds of goats and sheep by traversing their fields under the cover of overhanging brush and trees bordering the water.

Each night, Mac Craack pointed him to a sheltered place for rest, and the goat slept deeply and peacefully. Each day began at dawn, when Wonder would awake and raise his eyes to the growing light. Breathing slowly, he would repeat his mantra to himself several times as quiet grew within him. *Into the Light . . . into the Light . . . into the Light.*

One morning, he fell so deeply into the stillness that Mac Craack had to rap his beak sharply against the goat's muzzle to bring him back.

"Master mastering?" he inquired when Wonder roused. "Where is goat?"

Wonder eyed the crow as he rolled his head from side to side, easing the stiffness from his neck. "The Light leads downward and inward, Master Crow."

"GRAACK!" the crow responded. "Goat into Light? Or Light into goat?" The crow stepped close and peered at Wonder. "Where is goat?" he asked again.

As often happened since their return from the mountains, Presence surrounded them. And from it, a thought took form. "There is only Light, M.C. No matter outer appearances."

The crow cackled joyfully and flapped his glossy wings. "Where's goat?"

"No goat. Nothing but Light. Nothing but Presence."

"No wonder no goat," came the crow's quick response. With a leap, Mac Craack launched himself into the air and flew in an ever-widening circle overhead. It was time to continue the trek.

Late in the afternoon, the stream began to descend quickly through a notch in the land. Huge basalt ramparts grew all around as the water dropped into a deep, deep gorge. It grew very steep, and before long, Wonder could hear the great river as it crashed through the canyon.

He paused to gaze up and down the waterway, and then above. The river danced blue-green in the sunshine beneath the towering rock walls. Mac Craack hovered in thermal updrafts just overhead. Far above the crow, Wonder could see raptors spiraling. It was an extraordinary sight.

Clambering carefully he descended, sometimes reversing course to navigate around impassable sections, and came at last to a soft beach where the stream tumbled into the river. The waters surged through standing waves and crashing rapids, and Wonder felt humbled by its primal force.

He drank from the river and grazed on the grasses and shrubs that dotted its bank. Just as the sky darkened, he settled into a comfortable cleft. Mac Craack perched above him on a ledge. The sound of the river wrapped around Wonder, and he swiftly slid into a deep sleep.

A strange dream came to him just before he woke. It was dominated by the feeling of being squeezed through darkness. The pressure of moving through it was intense. It was as if all that preceded it had vanished. With its passing arose a sense of anticipation and newness. Wonder awoke with a start, a clear memory of the dream, and a word planted in his thoughts: *Initiative*.

Lost within himself, he contemplated the word. It made little sense to him, though he was certain its appearance in his mind was not an accident. Settling into quiet, he mentally recited his mantra. He knew the canyon was an outer passage that would squeeze him. Yet he sensed that what awaited him on the other side was even greater, a new life that would wholly swallow his old self. He breathed deeply, embracing it, welcoming it.

It was in this inner space that Lydia appeared to him once more. For a long time, he had carried with him a sense that she was close even though she had not appeared in his dreams again. This time was different. She was so near that it was almost indescribable, though again it was not in otter form but rather as spirit made tangible. There were no words, only the most comforting communion he could imagine. Their spirits hung together in stillness beyond words or thoughts, and even beyond corporeality. There was nothing else.

It felt like only moments, but when he emerged from inwardness, the gorge was bathed in pale, cool light that would last well into the day. Mac Craack was nowhere to be seen, so the goat browsed slowly. Sometime later, the crow returned, dropping onto the sand before Wonder.

"Master Goat masters rocks now! Climb on, climb over!"

"M.C., I believe that the rocks are masters unto themselves. Co-operation with them may be the best idea."

"GRAWWK! Wisdom and wonder, Master Wonder!"

Wonder told Mac Craack about both his sleeping and waking dreams. He did not seek an answer of any kind from the crow, and none was offered. Regardless, it was apparent that Mac Craack was very attentive.

After long moments, the crow nodded his head to acknowledge Wonder's inner work. "Into the Light, into Initiative. Goat cracked and cracking."

The day that followed was arduous. Fortunately, the canyon walls were steep enough that it shielded Wonder from the hot sun for most of the trek. Still, navigating the rocks was quite a test. The terrain challenged him continually as the trail moved steadily and steeply downhill. The river churned in rapids broken by more waterfalls than he could count.

With such intense focus required, Wonder had little time to notice anything other than each step. But throughout the day, he recalled the words Boboso the bear had spoken to him: *The path is every step*. That memory seemed lifetimes ago.

Just as the sunlight began to fade, the canyon opened into a great plain that rolled away as far as the eye could see. The river broadened and quieted beneath massive cottonwoods like a great silver snake sunning itself. Wonder sank gratefully into the tall grass, too weary even to graze.

It was then that Mac Craack chose to speak of the ocean to which the river would lead. Wonder had once asked to learn more. The crow had silenced him bluntly, "HERE, NOW!" Thankfully, Wonder knew the lesson of patience and simply trusted the time would come.

"Ocean," Mac Craack began dreamily. "Like plains, but watery. Like lake, but wavy."

"Why tell me now, M.C.?" Wonder asked as his head began to nod.

"Ebb and flow, Master Goat, ebb and flow."

With yet one more mysterious comment from his guide, the goat slept.

28

The Heart of the Plain

I T WAS FIRST LIGHT WHEN HE AWOKE. MAC CRAACK PERCHED on a slender branch, peering into Wonder's face. "Master Goat?" he croaked.

Wonder cracked open an eye. "Yes, Master Crow?"

"Come." And with that the crow took to the air. Though he swooped and gamboled in the breeze, he was careful to stay close enough for Wonder to see him. The goat forded shallows and crossed onto a sandbar, soaked up to his hocks.

Mac Craack landed beside him. "Watch," he said and pointed to the east with his beak.

Through a break in the trees lining the river, they could see the prairie, still pale in the darkness. The light steadily rose, and colors spread across the horizon, vanquishing the deep blue of night. Rays of light soared in the sky, and a moment later, the sun rose, round and glorious. Beneath it the grasses rippled like gold shimmering from within.

Wonder imagined he could feel his breath intertwined with the wind as he inhaled the magnificent sight.

"See, Master Goat." It was a statement, not a question. "Goat goes into the Light. Goat Initiates. Where is Light?"

"Everywhere, M.C., everywhere."

"RAWK!" Mac Craack lifted his wings and shook them vigorously, stirring a maelstrom of dust. "Beneath crow, earth flies. Always so. Always so."

The crow cocked his head and peered at Wonder. "Great people live near. They walk in beauty. See?"

The goat sighed wistfully. "The Light always appears as beauty."

"CRAAWK!" The squawked reply echoed long. "Just Light, Master Goat." The crow lowered his beak to peer again at the goat. "No dark. Just Light."

Wonder nodded his head very slowly. "We are never beyond the Light even when we cannot see it," he hazarded.

Mac Craack spun into the air without a word, and their trek resumed. The rest of the day was spent amid the quiet of the cottonwood forest flanking the river. And for several days more, the landscape changed little. The crow called it a bosque, a seemingly endless canopy of yellow-green leafy boughs atop stout trunks. Small creatures scurried everywhere, while a bounty of birds flitted overhead. Tufts of grass dotted the earth, and small channels of cool, clear water crisscrossed Wonder's path. At one point, the trees opened and offered a view of the river that was now so wide it stunned him. The bosque continued as far as he could see, no matter how long he walked.

One evening, the crow was especially careful in finding a place to rest for the night. Instead of flying off on his own pursuits as he usually did, Mac Craack roosted very near. When Wonder awoke, the crow was in exactly the same spot.

Wonder cocked his head and looked up at Mac Craack, who was already awake and watchful. "You've not moved, M.C. What's wrong?"

The crow nodded gravely. "Nearing city of men."

"And . . . ?"

Instead of answering him, Mac Craack turned his head and listened. Long moments passed.

"Danger. Do nothing." He paused. "Do nothing," he repeated, then launched into the air with a burst of black feathers. "GRAWK!"

The goat grazed and rested throughout the morning. If there was nothing to be done, then there was nothing to do. A short time later, he was dozing in the warm morning sun.

Mac Craack did not return until early evening. By then, Wonder was nervous with energy. Many days of action had primed him for motion. While resting was beneficial, it left him ready to move.

"CRAWK," announced the bird upon alighting. "Go goat?"

Wonder chortled. "Yes M.C., I'm ready to go."

Under a bright wedge of moon, their trek began anew.

29

City of Men

As the night lengthened, Mac Craack flew low and close so Wonder could follow him easily. They wove through the cottonwoods with occasional diversions around thick undergrowth and brambles.

All the while, Wonder could sense the growing mechanical buzz of the city. With one part of his attention on the crow and the path unfolding before him, another probed this new and unfamiliar feeling of human energy. In keeping with his learning, he accepted it as neither good nor bad though it had a distinctly different feel from anything he was used to. Humans at the farm were one thing; this was another.

Just before sunrise, he was aware of a thinning of the bosque as human dwellings began to encroach on the gallery of forest. Loud noises began to penetrate the quiet sanctity of the trees and burbling waters. And at dawn, Wonder heard the voices of men.

It was then that Mac Craack, who had spoken little throughout the night, croaked directions that led to a dense copse of willows heavily fringed with river grasses. It was nearly impenetrable, and were it not for a few tunnels wandering beneath the growth, Wonder would never have been able to enter. Deep within this protective mantle, he settled. Mac Craack again croaked, as near to a whisper as possible for a crow, "Ranger. Danger!" Then he perched high in the branches to keep watch.

Strange noises periodically punctured his web of seclusion. He could barely contain his curiosity at some of the mechanical sounds:

roaring in the sky overhead, distant grinding noises that reverberated across the river, an occasional clank or shouting voice. Yet Mac Craack's earlier warning kept him quiet and concealed.

By early afternoon, his need to move pressed him to his feet. "M.C.?" he whispered into the branches that overhung his hiding place.

The crow had flown away to reconnoiter. Wonder decided to have a look around and slowly worked his way through the undergrowth. Emerging by the riverbank, he poked his head out to survey this new world.

Downriver, he could see a very large bridge spanning the water. Large, shiny metal boxes moved speedily across it like beetles scurrying on a log. Upriver, a collection of huge chimneys released thin clouds into the air. He could just make out structures on the other side of the trees, many times larger than the barn he had grown up in.

Wonder stepped forward a few feet and stopped to breathe it all in. Quieting his mind and softening his sight, he slowly turned his head. Wave after wave of sensation rose and fell in and through him. The curiosity upon which he thrived was both satisfied by this new experience and further piqued. He had to see more of this strange new world.

Moving slowly, he eased upstream toward the edge of the thicket. Cornering the brush, he scanned the banks of the river. He was so attentive to the experience and its reflection within him that he did not notice the group of men. A shout drew him back, and peering through the trees, he saw them. One was pointing directly toward him. They were dressed alike in muted uniforms that faded into the terrain. As he watched, they spread out, encircling the area of dense undergrowth in which he had sheltered.

Tense with fear, Wonder scanned the skies in search of Mac Craack. The bird was nowhere in sight. He looked to the water as his best route of escape. Shallow for the most part, it had a channel of deep water that would be a challenge, but he saw that he could use the current to speed his flight.

Quieting himself, he listened inwardly. Thoughts arose, and he announced them to himself out loud. "Initiative. And the path is every step."

Wonder bolted in a burst of energy.

For a single moment, he thought the movement had freed him. Then something stung his haunch. Another dozen strides passed before he felt himself losing control of his body. He tried harder but soon tumbled. As he rolled onto the ground and tried to lift his head, he saw Mac Craack circling overhead, screeching in alarm.

30

A TIME TO BE LOST

CONSCIOUSNESS RETURNED IN EBBS AND FLOWS. WONDER WAS first aware of darkness. Was it nighttime already? When his awareness next stirred, he felt a blanket of straw beneath a body that still felt sluggish and numb. He vaguely heard the subtle sounds of other creatures around him. He tried to lift himself to look around but could not.

An otherworldly vision came to him then. Oren looked down upon him. There was a twinkle in the old goat's yellow eyes as he spoke without the movement of his mouth. "My dear Wonder, this is most certainly an interesting detour. Remember, there is no path that is not in the Light. The secret is in what you do with the path that finds you."

The vision slipped away as Wonder again lost consciousness.

The next thing he knew, the darkness had grayed into morning, and his head felt like a hollowed-out gourd. As he rolled up, he found he was able to stand, albeit awkwardly. Staggering around like a newborn kid, he surveyed his surroundings. He was in an old, barnlike structure, filled with bales of hay and an odd collection of creatures large and small, including a dozen or more goats.

From the rafters, he heard a familiar croak. "Wonder wondering?"

He looked up to find Mac Craack peering down at him. The bird was a welcome sight in this strange place.

"Where am I?" he asked, his voice slurred so all the words all ran together. Wonder shook his head to clear it, and as he did, he discovered that something metal had been clipped into his right ear. He turned in a tight half circle, trying to see what the jangling thing was.

"Calm, calmer, calmest," croaked Mac Craack.

Wonder closed his eyes and breathed deeply for a few moments. *Remember the Light. Remember the Light.* The barn smelled not unlike the one he had grown up in, rich with hay and the aroma of goats, but there were other, unfamiliar smells too. Many creatures had trod this floor before him, he realized. He opened his eyes and approached the knot of fellow goats nearby. They were huddled together, and Wonder intuited it to be as much for warmth as the comfort of closeness. While he well understood the need for companions and camaraderie, he felt a flood of gratitude arise from within, not for their presence but rather in response to the certainty that all was well with him no matter the circumstance. Even in this strange situation, he knew deep inside that he had achieved great freedom from dependence upon others. Returning from his momentary reverie, he saw that the goats were eyeing him warily, their long, slatted pupils wide in the semi-darkness.

"Greetings, friends," said Wonder, bowing his head and sweeping one hoof in a broad arc, as was proper when meeting a stranger. "My name is Wonder, but I am not that. Tell me, where is this place and why have we been brought here?"

The goats looked to each other and then back at Wonder a number of times. Finally, one of them, a young nanny with a cream-colored coat mottled with chocolate spots, spoke. "We were grazing by a big water, but then the men came and now we are here. Soon, we will be somewhere else. Or not."

She blinked at him very, very slowly. Wonder wasn't sure if whatever drug had caused him to fall into a stupor was still affecting her or if that was just her natural disposition. He nodded his thanks and rejoined Mac Craack.

"I don't think they know anything," he said, folding his legs and sinking to the straw. "M.C., I know there are unknowns at every turn, and yet I would be a fool not to question whether I should have ever left the pasture."

The crow hopped down from his perch and landed on Wonder's shoulder. He ran his black beak through the goat's white coat, preening him as if he were a fledgling, and then pecked at the jangling metal thing in Wonder's ear.

"Ow!" cried Wonder.

"RAWWWK!" called the crow. The raucous sound snapped the goat even more into awareness. "No time for sorrow-full goat. Rest now, regret never."

"Regret never." Wonder contemplated the feel of the phrase. "M.C., I cannot think of truer words at this moment."

Wonder brought his attention to bear on heeding the crow's advice. All around him, he heard the quiet rustlings of his fellow captives as they awoke. Some bleated in alarm, others whimpered. A voice cried out, over and over again, for its mother. Wonder turned his focus inward, carefully noticing and rejecting each inner urge to worry, and waited for whatever the coming day would bring.

31

THREE NANNIES

SEVERAL DAYS LATER, MEN ARRIVED JUST AFTER DAWN AND herded the animals into large metal crates. The floor was hard, and the air was stale, but Wonder could glimpse the dark blot of feathers that was Mac Craack through the small holes punched into the walls of his new prison. With him were several other goats, all of them much smaller and darker than his old herd mates. They did not seem interested in conversation, and Wonder soon gave up trying to talk to them.

Regardless, the experience gave him ideas with which to play. He had discovered that some creatures were profoundly Awake. Oren had been one such creature, as was the mighty Boboso and a handful of others Wonder had met in the course of his travels. Then there were the creatures that had Awakened to a lesser degree. His Maa and Paa, dear though they were to him, fell into this category. From there, it was apparent that many others were just deaf to their own inner nature. There was no fault to be found; it was simply the way of things.

He was jolted back to the present moment when the crate lurched forward with a roar like a great beast. The other goats went rigid and toppled over. Wonder hurried over to see if he could help them, but within seconds, they were upright once more as if nothing had happened. Each time the enclosure shook or bounced, the little goats again stiffened and fell. Wonder soon learned to ignore it, for the experience didn't seem to do them any harm. It was as if their fear struck them into unconsciousness, which was a great curiosity.

Wonder turned his attention to the scene outside the crate. He pressed his eye to one of the peepholes and looked out at the swiftly moving landscape beyond. It reminded him a little of the sensation of flight he'd experienced so long ago when the owl had snatched him from the earth. Now he was flying swiftly, faster than any bird or beast, and very low to the ground. He reminded himself that this was all part of a great adventure, and for an instant, he was rewarded with a feeling of awe and excitement.

Sometimes his view was blocked by other metal boxes speeding past. They swooped and swerved, blared and bellowed. Inside them were people, and Wonder thought it sad that they too were captives of these infernal devices.

Unable to see the sun, he had no sense of how much time passed. At last, the container stopped moving. The sudden absence of momentum seemed to startle the other goats, and once more they fell over, their legs sticking straight out into the air. The men opened the back of the metal box and let down a ramp. One of them tossed a loop of rope around Wonder's neck, and he had no choice but to follow.

The man led him through a maze of concrete corridors. There were no green things in this place, no soft turf beneath his hooves, and despite Master Oren's reminder that all paths are of the Light, he felt tendrils of despair tugging at his insides.

Soon, they passed through a set of metal doors, and Wonder found himself blinking in bright, warm, sunlight. The man handed the end of the rope to another human, a woman in khaki shorts who smiled and patted Wonder on the head.

"Is this the one that was in the woods near the river?" she asked. "How did he get there?"

"Beats me. Must have got loose from someone's farm. The rangers were looking for wild dogs someone complained about, but the goat was all they could find."

The woman handed the man some pieces of paper. He nodded and walked away without another glance. Wonder did not understand their speech, and he felt mystified at the proceedings.

The woman took him to a small, grassy paddock with a fence. There was a miniature barn, just big enough for a few goats to shelter in, a bale of sweet hay and a trough of fodder, and several basins of water. She took the rope from his neck and patted him on the head once more. After the woman left, Wonder nibbled on the hay and found it to be tasty, if a trifle dry. The water tasted fine, but it was nothing compared with the icy streams he'd drunk from in the wild. In the barn, he was surprised to find the sleepy-eyed, cream-colored nanny he'd met earlier, along with two other goats he'd never seen before. She smiled up at him in a vague sort of way.

"Hello again, Miss," he said politely.

She blinked at him. "Oh, hello, Wonder-not-Wonder. I told you we'd be somewhere else soon, and here we are."

"Er, yes. Here we are. And what might your name be?"

"I am called Serena. This is Hazel," she said, pointing her snout at the light brown goat with drooping ears to her left. She turned to the nanny on her right, a gray goat with a white streak down her back. "This is Lucinda. They're here. Now we're here too. Hazel says that there used to be another buck here, but he went away."

The goat called Hazel nodded. "Norman was a nasty old thing," she said.

Lucinda chimed in. "Oh yes, always butting his horns against the fence and keeping all the hay to himself. He bit a small boy once, you know."

"The boys and girls bring us biscuits," said Hazel. "They taste nice. The biscuits, that is. I never bit anyone. That was Norman."

"You look like a nice goat," said Lucinda. "Not like that Norman."

"Girls," said Serena, "aren't we lucky to be here with this nice goat and those nice biscuits and this nice barn?"

"Oh yes," said Lucinda and Hazel together.

Wonder backed away slowly. Their inane chatter felt like the buzzing of bees in his ears, and their bland acceptance of their surroundings made him realize he'd been insufficiently attentive to his own curious nature. He nodded respectfully to each of the nannies in turn and went to see what else he might find in this strange, new place.

32

INSIDE JOB

WONDER COULD SEE FOUR OTHER ENCLOSURES FROM HIS paddock. His nearest neighbors were a pair of grumpy burros who reminded him of Mr. and Mrs. Mule back home, and a small heard of petite, dark-haired goats. He recognized some of them as the fainting goats who had traveled with him to this place. Sure enough, every time there was a loud noise or a sudden movement nearby, the little goats fell over with their legs sticking straight up into the air.

When he asked their names, they told him they were all called Kevin.

"It cuts down on the confusion," explained one of them. "We mislike to be confused. Or upstartled. Or upset in any way. It's like me Granny Kevin always said: 'Kevin, don't make life harder than it is.'"

Across the way, there was a much larger fenced-in yard with a row of wooden lean-tos and a number of fuzzy white sheep that looked like clouds with legs, as well as tall, long-necked creatures that Wonder had never seen before. Juanita, one of the burros, later told him they were cousins of the sheep called llamas. The sheep and llamas were too far away for conversation, but Wonder enjoyed watching them. The llamas, in particular, were fascinating, like sheep that had been stretched out. He wished he could chat with them since they seemed to be remarkably peaceful. He imagined they would understand inner attention.

The farthest paddock was the most interesting of all. Wonder had to stand with his front hooves on the fence and crane his neck to see it, but the effort was worth it. Two enormous birds with long, sweeping tails strutted there, their plumage glittering green and blue and gold. The colors reminded him of the sun-drenched grassy valleys he'd seen on his journey, crisscrossed with ribbons of blue water beneath an even bluer sky.

Sometimes the beautiful birds screamed for no reason, and each time their raucous cry split the air, the little goats in the neighboring pen fainted. The Kevins also fainted when the woman in khaki shorts returned with a wheelbarrow full of fodder, and again when Lupita, Juanita's sister, belched loudly after lunch. It was a mystery how the goats could survive, let alone enjoy full lives, when at any moment they might blank out. Yet Wonder knew by now that there were many ways of being in the world, and none was better or worse than another. The Kevins, for their part, seemed to take their fainting episodes in stride.

That afternoon, Wonder nearly fainted himself when a ball of black feathers fell from the sky and landed on a post just inches from his nose. He greeted the crow joyfully.

"M.C.! I wondered about your absence," he said once he had mastered his emotions.

The crow flexed his wings in an apparent shrug. "Goat not done. Mac Craack not done."

"I'm afraid I *am* done," said Wonder. He looked around at the enclosures. "Juanita—she's the burro over there—told me she and her sister have been here for at least six summers. I . . . I don't think I'm ever getting out of here."

"Maybe, maybe not," said Mac Craack, as cryptic as ever. "Forgot Boboso?"

The goat contemplated the bear's words from what now seemed a lifetime ago. "Ah. The path is made with every step."

"GRAWWK!" the crow affirmed.

"And this is the path right here. Right now."

With those words, a profound quiet fell into the space that surrounded Wonder and Mac Craack. The goat felt his concerns vanish in response to what he knew to be the truth. That was the secret to the Light of Awareness: All fear vanished in its Presence.

Unbidden, he heard himself say, "We get what we get."

"Get! Got! Goat!" the crow chortled. "Wise goat?"

Wonder laughed. "Yes, M.C. I am."

Wonder introduced him to Serena, Hazel, and Lucinda, who stopped gossiping just long enough to say hello. They chattered together as if they had known each other since they were kids, seemingly content to be wherever they were. Juanita and Lupita inclined their long, narrow heads in greeting, and the crow said something to them in Spanish that made the burros bray with laughter. The sound made the fainting goats fall over, and when they roused themselves a few moments later, the crow's mischievous cry of "CRAACK!" caused them to faint all over again. Mac Craack repeated the trick with great amusement.

"Craacked goats," he concluded.

The crow told Wonder that he'd done a flyover of the area and seen many other animals, like brown bears nearly as big as Boboso and otters as playful as Lydia. There were other creatures that even Mac Craack had never seen before, huge scaly things that lived in the water and giant striped cats that lazed in the sun. There were tall, spotted creatures whose long necks put the llamas to shame and a trio of giant beasts that Mac Craack said looked like walking mountains with two tails, one in front and the other in back. The goat had heard their trumpeting cry, and he wondered if he'd ever get to see them for himself.

The crow also told Wonder the name of his new home: Roca Plana Zoo.

Wonder cocked his head to one side. "What's a 'zoo,' MC?"

The crow croaked, "Cages. Clipped wings. Craack!"

"Then this is to be my fate?" asked Wonder heavily. "I fear I will never see the ocean now, M.C. But it's not just that . . . it's more that my adventure may forever be incomplete."

Mac Craack studied Wonder with bright black eyes and then edged right up in front of the goat's muzzle. "Woe-full goat," he said at last. "Loss is loss is loss. Not to be denied. Still, much to see, to find, to be! Inside job, inside job! Infinite adventure."

The crow took flight and wheeled in a circle overhead, still cawing "Inside job!" as he flew.

33

LIFE IN ROCA PLANA

WONDER SOON LEARNED THAT A ZOO WAS A PLACE WHERE humans came to look at animals, and where animals in turn could look at them. The little ones would run up to pet him and his fellow captives and to hold out biscuits, which were not nearly as tasty as Hazel had said they were.

Sometimes when Wonder would reach out to take the offered treat, the child would squeal in delight or fear and retreat. Others tried to grab his horns or pull the short, silky beard that grew from his chin. A few stayed by the fences, quietly observing the animals with bright, solemn eyes until their parents pulled them on to the next exhibit.

Mac Craack told him that in other parts of the zoo, the humans and animals were separated by taller fences, wire mesh cages, or deep pits that could not be crossed. The goat wondered if the barriers were to protect the humans from the animals, or if it might not be the other way around. It was curious that the humans were allowed to interact with some of the animals and not others. He guessed it had to do with the potential for harm. That was something to consider, though he thought the humans might not have the right of it.

One day, some weeks after Wonder had arrived, a little boy dropped his ice cream cup just inside the burros' enclosure. His parents were distracted by the herd of fainting goats, and did not see him climb the fence and drop down the other side to retrieve it. Juanita and Lupita brayed in alarm, a crowd of humans rushed over, and several climbed over the fence to rescue him. When the boy noticed the ruckus he'd caused, he burst into loud, sticky tears. He was unharmed, of course; the burro sisters were gentle beneath their gruff exterior. But the boy's parents acted as though the child had been rescued from grave peril. The next day, two men came and put a wire mesh screen across all of the fences, and Wonder felt as though his world had grown just a little bit smaller.

Otherwise, Wonder's new life was entirely uneventful. His trek to the sea was, it seemed, at an end. At first, the activity to which he had become accustomed caused him to pace the length of his enclosure so much that his hooves wore a narrow track in the turf. As time passed, though, he gradually grew less restless. When he would find himself pacing once more, Wonder turned his attention inward, inhabiting the vast space within himself, and he would be at peace for a while.

Over and over, he would remind himself there was only Light, and that for now, this was his path. It was sometimes a frustrating practice. The goat became increasingly aware of the hundreds of ways discontent could arise without warning. Many were surprisingly subtle, like the day the nannies had been laughing yet again at some inane story. Wonder felt dislike bubble up from nowhere. Immediately, he named it as a lie, and it fell away to be replaced once more with quiet contentment. He made note of the experience and continued to pay attention to any negative urges as they arose.

Fortunately, Mac Craack was a steady presence. Though the crow often flew off on his own mysterious pursuits, he never stayed away for long. He roosted in the rafters of the tiny barn at night, and by day, he perched on the fencepost near Wonder. Together, they observed the world, only occasionally remarking on what they saw. It was almost the same companionable quiet Wonder had enjoyed with Oren, but the crow tended to cackle to himself as if he'd just thought of a clever joke he wasn't ready to share yet.

Wonder thought of his old teacher often. He knew in his heart that Oren had passed from this world, but more important, he knew that Oren lived on through Wonder's memories. The goat tried to teach the other animals of the zoo using Oren's methods, but he did not have much success.

"See how the sheep and the llamas keep to themselves on opposite sides of their paddock?" he asked Juanita and Lupita one day. "You said they were cousins, so why do you suppose there is such division?"

But the burros only snorted and returned to their feed trough.

He tried again with the three nannies. "Do you smell that crispness in the air? The cold season is fast approaching. Do you think it will rain this afternoon, or will the clouds hold out until night?"

But the nanny goats just looked at him, their heads cocked to the side at precisely the same angle, and then returned to their gossip.

Finally, he tried to teach the herd of fainting goats in the neighboring paddock. "See that beetle—" he began.

"What, where!" cried one of the goats, and they all fell stiff-legged to the ground.

And so Wonder stopped trying to teach them. Instead, he spent more and more time in quiet contemplation. When he sometimes overheard the other goats remarking on how strange it was that Wonder just stood there staring at nothing all the time, he smiled to himself. He realized that he must appear to them as Oren had to his herd: a goat apart.

One quiet afternoon when no humans were around, Wonder discussed discontent with Mac Craack. "M.C., I have watched discontent appear out of nothingness. And I don't seem to be unique; it seems to be the same for all creatures. Am I on track, then?"

"GRAWK! Tracked goat."

"I'm guessing that doesn't change; we are always susceptible to such bubbling negativity. Even you, Master Crow."

Mac Craack gave a curt nod as if to encourage Wonder.

"So the only option we have is to notice the inner shifts as they arise, name them, and release them."

"CRAACK! Oren smiling. Wise, wise goat."

"Do you have such urgings, M.C.?"

"Seldom seen, Wonder not wonder."

With that, the crow launched into the air, leaving Wonder with a renewed certainty that he was indeed on the path.

From that day forward, whenever Mac Craack left on one of his avian errands, Wonder settled into the rhythm of his own breath. He stood stock-still for hours while overhead the sun slowly rose and then sank. If he was lucky, sometimes he met Presence there.

There is a stone in my path, thought Wonder, deep within the cool, quiet space where Presence dwelt. *I have not gone where I meant to go. I got what I got.*

And after a little time—though time was difficult to gauge in that place—Presence responded: *The only way out is through.*

34

OLIVIA

WONDER RESOLVED TO MAKE PEACE WITH HIS LIFE. His path had taken him far from where he intended to go, but if he was destined to be in this place, he would inhabit it as fully as he could for as long as he was there.

All paths lead into the Light, he reminded himself. *And since I am here, I might as well be present.*

As he thought this, he wondered if something of Serena was rubbing off on him. She was always content no matter what, and while at first, he had thought her incurious or even simple-minded, he now suspected that she was quite wise in her own way. Of course, it was also possible she did not experience as he did, but it really didn't matter how a creature found peace—only that it did.

As he grew to accept his fate, Wonder also began to embrace his role in the zoo. With quiet dignity, he allowed the children to pat his head and touch his horns. He ate the biscuits they offered, not because he was hungry or because they were particularly tasty, but because it gave the visitors such delight. As for the quiet children, the ones who hung back shyly just beyond the fences, he gave them the time and space and peace to watch him until their fear drained away and they felt brave enough to approach. When they did, he lowered his head solemnly and let them touch his wiry white coat.

To his surprise, Wonder discovered that human children were often inquisitive and delightful. They reminded him of himself when he was a kid. And appreciation came to him, or at least that was what Mac Craack called the warm generous feelings. Before now, his experience with humans had been limited. The man who ran the farm where Wonder grew up was only a shadowy presence in his memory, and the only other men he'd encountered were the ones who'd captured him.

Now he saw hundreds of men and women, as well as their offspring, every day. They were noisy and often smelled like artificial flowers or trees, and they dripped sticky drinks and treats everywhere they went, but they also were curious and filled with laughter. Especially the children. They giggled and squealed like otter kits, always rushing about to see the next thing and then the next.

One day, a petite older girl with a sleek brown bob the color of silt and merry brown eyes approached his paddock. She walked over to Wonder, ignoring the antics of the fainting goats and the three nannies jockeying for position at the fence, and held out her slender hand. When the nannies saw she wasn't holding a biscuit, they lost interest, but Wonder trotted over, intrigued.

"Hello," she said brightly. "My name's Olivia. What's yours?"

The goat gazed up into her eyes and let out a sigh. "Wonder," he said, and she smiled as if she understood him. Her eyes sparkled like sunlight on water, and Wonder stared up into them, entranced. He felt a jolt of energy as a connection crackled between them.

"Do I . . . do I know you?" asked Wonder.

The girl smiled again and nodded. "That's right," she said, scratching him beneath the chin. "Aren't you a handsome fellow?"

Olivia stayed by the fence, speaking quietly to Wonder, while all around the peacocks screamed and the burros brayed and the other children ran back and forth squealing in delight. After a while, Mac Craack fluttered down to peer at the girl. She greeted him politely, and to Wonder's great surprise, the crow bowed his sleek black head and let Olivia stroke his feathers.

"Took you long enough," the crow muttered, his eyes half closed.

"What a fine bird," Olivia cooed. She ran a finger lightly

through the feathers of his breast. Mac Craack bore this with evident enjoyment for a moment before fluttering a few feet away. He cackled to himself good-naturedly as he put the feathers she'd ruffled back in place.

"M.C., do you know this girl?" Wonder asked.

The bird paused in his grooming to fix one beady eye on Wonder. "Don't you?"

35

AN ORDINARY GOAT

OLIVIA STAYED FOR OVER AN HOUR ON THAT FIRST VISIT. SHE sat beside the fence and chattered merrily, telling Wonder and Mac Craack about her family and her schooling and her pony, who was called Pepper. She assured Wonder that he and Pepper would be good friends. She shared an apple with Wonder—it was far tastier than the crumbly biscuits or sweet hay he usually had, and the goat ate his half in two bites. Olivia giggled and promised to bring him another next week.

When at last Olivia's parents came to collect her, she stood with reluctance and patted Wonder again before being led away. While her mother fussed over the dirt on the girl's jeans, her father said, "Come on, Livvie. Wouldn't you rather see the tigers or the elephants? That's just an ordinary goat."

As Wonder watched the girl depart, he felt sadness shadow his heart. The world seemed to lose a little of its color in her absence, and he looked up to Mac Craack. "How long is a week?" he asked.

The crow chuckled and flapped his wings, as if whisking the question away on the breeze. "Time, no time," said the crow. "The wheel turns and turns again."

And with that cryptic statement, he launched into the air and flew away.

Wonder continued to stand by the fence, watching the people pass by. They reminded him of the way the schools of fish had darted together in the clear streams he'd crossed, or perhaps of the nervous colony of prairie dogs he'd encountered. Although the crowd was made of individuals, it moved as one great beast with a mind of its own. He decided to share this observation with Mac Craack.

Some time later, Serena came sidling up to him and nudged him with her nose.

Wonder gave a little bleat, startled from his reverie. "Oh, hello," he said, bowing as was proper to a young lady goat.

She blinked slowly and asked, "Did that girl give you something nice to eat?"

"Yes," he admitted. "An apple. It was good."

"Apples are good."

They stood in silence for a little while longer. Wonder was never quite sure what to say around Serena. She was pretty, with a cream-colored coat, long eyelashes, and petite hooves, and sometimes Wonder noticed her staring at him with languid, dreamy eyes. Whenever he caught her gaze, she would look away, and a moment later, he would hear the other nannies erupt into tittering laughter.

Abruptly, Serena said, "Would you like to be my mate?"

Wonder blinked. Surely he had misheard her. "Excuse me?"

"Well," said Serena, leaning her flank against his, "you're a billy and I'm a nanny. Isn't that how these things work?"

Wonder took a step to the side, away from Serena. He was pro-foundly glad that Mac Craack was not here to see this. "Er, yes. I mean, usually, but I don't—"

"You're a nice buck," Serena pressed, "and I'm a healthy young she-goat. I could give you many fine kids."

"Look, Serena—"

"Do you like one of the other nannies better? Lucinda is too old, and Hazel is too stout. They wouldn't be good for you, not like me."

"But I—"

"It's what goats *do*," she insisted. "We grow up, find a mate, and have kids of our own. My mammy always told me to find a nice buck to settle down with. You're . . . you're my only hope for a fam-ily, Wonder-not-Wonder. Please?"

Wonder's first impulse was to bolt, but he was trapped in the enclosure with Serena and the other nannies. A very small part of him even considered accepting her offer. Would it be so bad, after all, to settle down and raise a couple of kids with a pretty she-goat? He could teach them all he knew and carry on Oren's legacy.

And his kids would grow up in a cage.

Wonder shook his head. "I'm sorry, Serena. You really are very nice, but I don't want a mate. Not you, not Lucinda or Hazel. No offense! I may be stuck in here, but I won't have any kids of mine imprisoned with me."

Serena's eyes narrowed, and she blew out twin puffs of air through her nostrils. Without another word, she walked stiffly back to the other two nannies and knelt on the ground beside them. They whispered together, their heads bowed, and Wonder knew they were talking about him.

"Let them gossip," he said aloud. Wonder knew, even if Serena and the others had not realized it, that any hope they had for a normal life had ended the moment they were brought to this place. Perhaps if he'd been any other goat, he would have accepted her offer anyway, but Oren had taught him better than that. He wouldn't let himself be distracted by a passing fancy or be lulled asleep by creature comforts. Wonder was Awake in ways that Serena would never be, and he understood now that he would always be a goat apart.

Later that evening, when Mac Craack returned and alit on a nearby fencepost, Wonder told him what had happened. The crow, for once, restrained himself from cackling or making wry remarks while Wonder spoke.

"Did I make the right decision?" Wonder asked when his tale was told.

The crow shrugged his wings. Wonder hadn't really expected an answer. He looked inward for a time, examining his feelings as if they were a collection of polished stones. He found a little pebble of disappointment there, as well as frustration and embarrassment and worry and even homesickness. He named each one and set it aside. Those feelings were part of him, but they did not define him anymore than his name did.

"Sometimes I *do* wish I was just an ordinary goat with an ordinary life," Wonder admitted after a long silence. "But that was never going to be my path. I see that now. I may not see and do all I wanted to in this turn of the wheel, but I have made my peace with it."

"Extra-ordinary," mused Mac Craack. "Extra goat is more goat, nay?"

Despite his brief melancholy, Wonder laughed.

36

THE ZOOKEEPER

THINGS WERE AWKWARD BETWEEN WONDER AND THE NANNY goats for a while after Serena's proposal. The trio gave him dark looks, and whenever he tried to approach the fodder trough in their corner of the paddock, they crowded him out, turning their backs to him and pressing their flanks so he couldn't pass.

Wonder bore this treatment with good grace, despite the crow's cracks at his expense. As the weather turned colder, however, Serena's frosty attitude thawed. The other two nannies followed her lead, as they did in most things. Gradually, life went back to the way it had been before: the trio of nannies stayed in the shade of the barn near the troughs and gossiped all day, while Wonder stood at the fence, steadily studying and contemplating the world beyond the enclosure.

Long hours passed during which Wonder simply watched the leaves of the nearby trees turn golden and then fall. The humans who tended the zoo scooped up the leaves almost as soon as they fell, almost as if they wanted to erase any evidence of the turning seasons. It made Wonder feel even more as if he were trapped in a place outside of time, and the shadows that continued to seek to command his heart grew greater.

The woman in the khaki shorts appeared occasionally to check on him and the other animals in the petting zoo. She was short and plump, with a broad, red-cheeked face and frizzing hair the color of dust. Whenever she visited, she spoke kindly to each of the animals in turn, ruffling their feathers or stroking their hair, and cooing in an almost-musical way that set even the high-strung fainting goats at ease.

The woman, who Mac Craack said was a zookeeper, checked his ears and hooves, brushed through his coat to check for ticks and other parasites, and shone a light into his eyes that made him try to jerk his head out of her strong, brown hands. Sometimes she stung him with a silver needle that left his flank sore for hours. Once, she looped a rope around his neck and led him through the concrete tunnels, and Wonder struggled to quiet the furious beating of his heart. Was she letting him go?

His disappointment was like a physical weight when, instead of releasing him, the zookeeper simply had him stand on a metal platform for a few moments before leading him back to the petting zoo.

"We've got to fatten you up," she said as she poured out an extra portion of fodder. "You're too skinny by half."

Wonder waited until she was gone, then indicated to Serena, Hazel, and Lucinda that they were welcome to share in this unexpected bounty.

One evening, she lingered by Wonder's enclosure after her inspection of the goats was over. She leaned against the fence and mopped her brow with a red handkerchief that was almost the same color as her face. After a moment, Wonder walked up and stood beside her, and the two of them looked out over the fence together. Mac Craack fluttered down onto the fencepost, and the zookeeper's eyebrows shot up into her frizzy hair.

"What's with you, crow?" she asked. "I see you here almost every day."

Mac Craack answered with his best cackle. "Craacked today, craacked tomorrow," he said, doing a little two-step that was most unbirdlike.

The zookeeper blinked and rubbed her eyes. "I think I'm working too hard," she muttered. "I know that crows are supposed to be smart, but it almost seems like you can understand me."

"Stand under!" he croaked. With a swirl of black wings, he rose into the air, crying, "Up, up, up and away!" as he flew.

Wonder chuckled at the crow's antics. Mac Craack's sense of humor never ceased to amuse him. The zookeeper shook her head and said, "Definitely working too hard."

She wiped her palms on her khaki shorts and unlatched the gate. When she left, Wonder saw that it had accidentally not latched behind her.

The gate was open.

37

MIDNIGHT WANDER

WONDER MADE HIMSELF WAIT UNTIL NIGHTFALL. IF HE WAS to escape, he reasoned, it would be best to go about it carefully. A mad dash in the daylight could only lead to a swift capture and return to his pen.

He waited in his usual spot by the fence, watching anxiously in case the woman in khaki shorts returned to latch the gate. The sun sank low in the sky, dipping below the horizon in a blaze of orange and pink, and the animals turned in for the night. Juanita and Lupita lay down beneath the branches of their favorite tree, and the herd of Kevins dropped to the ground and slept where they fell. Serena, Hazel, and Lucinda retired to the barn. Wonder briefly considered telling the nannies that the gate was open, but he didn't think they would come with him. Nor did he truly want them to.

While he waited for the cover of darkness, Wonder scanned the sky for Mac Craack, but the crow was nowhere to be found. It seemed he would have to make his escape alone.

Wonder took one last glance around, making sure no one was watching him, and then gently butted his horns against the unlatched gate. It swung open with a slight groan that made him freeze, holding his breath. After a tense, silent moment, he slipped through the opening.

He had no idea how to navigate the concrete tunnels through which he'd been led, so Wonder set about doing what he did best: exploring. His path was illuminated by dim orange lights high up on what appeared to be metal trees. They peered down at him like the glowing eyes of predators. Wonder paused by the enclosure where the peacocks lived, but he couldn't get a good look at the jewel-colored birds. Beyond their pen was undiscovered territory.

He followed his instincts and trotted along first one path and then another. His sensitive nose was met by many different, confusing smells. He heard the snores of great beasts and the sound of running water, but through the lush, dark leaves of the trees and shrubs, he could see nothing.

"If I follow the path," he panted, "I must eventually reach the exit. Just stay on the path. The only way out is through."

Wonder repeated this mantra as he first walked, then trotted, and then ran. But his path dead-ended at a large, low building. He turned and went back the way he had come until he reached a fork in the path. He followed it to the left and found himself at the edge of a large, rocky enclosure surrounded by a high fence. Several of the orange lights were clustered here, making it easy to see inside the pen.

"Hello?" he called out tentatively. "Is anyone there?"

One of the rocks began to move. A creature as large as a barn stood before him on tree-trunk legs. It had a long whippy tail in back and an even longer, thicker one in front. This, he realized, was one of the elephants Mac Craack had told him about. The elephant flapped its fan-shaped ears and lumbered toward Wonder. The goat felt the impact of its feet as a tremor in the earth, and he shied back.

"Be not afraid," said the elephant in a surprisingly high, fluting voice. "I will not step on you, small one."

"Hello, sir," said Wonder. "My name is Wonder, but I am not that."

"And I am Ronan," said the elephant. "How come you to be here? Should you not be with your kind elsewhere in Roca Plana?"

Wonder shook his head. "I am looking for the way out."

The elephant's ears flapped again, and his long front tail swung back and forth. "No, no, no," he crooned. "No way out but one, and you do not want to go that way."

"What way is that?"

Ronan the elephant lowered his head. "Death, little one. The only way any of us can get out of here is if we're too old or sick to be on display any longer. We of the Broken Tusk Herd have long memories, and I have seen generations of beasts led into the dark tunnels."

Wonder's heart sank. "Is there truly no other way out?"

"Not that I know," said Ronan. "But perhaps Lady Beryl might. Her memory is even longer than mine. You might ask her."

Ronan told Wonder where to find Lady Beryl. Wonder thanked him and set out in search of answers.

38

THE LADY BERYL

WONDER FOLLOWED RONAN'S DIRECTIONS. THE PATH twisted and turned, and soon he found himself at a large circle where three other paths intersected. At the center of the circle was a small mountain surrounded by water. Where the water met the lower slope, a dozen long, plump forms rested. Wonder crept forward for a better look.

One of the forms shifted and raised its head. The creature had a wide, whiskered face with heavy jowls and vast, dark eyes. Its body was a sleek muscular cylinder that ended in a broad tail. Raising itself up on its flippers, the creature gazed down at Wonder imperiously.

"Who," it intoned in a deep voice, "are you?"

It was on the tip of his tongue to say "My name is Wonder, but I am not that," but Wonder found himself tongue-tied in the presence of the obviously powerful creature. It had almost the size and strength of Boboso the bear but also had the sleekness of the otters. There was something about it that filled him with awe—and a little fear.

"You may call me Wonder," said the goat, bowing low. "I have come to see Beryl."

"And you may call me Rosalind," said the great beast. "I will let my lady know you are here. Wait where you are, little one."

Wonder, more curious than ever, waited. After a few minutes, a shape even larger than that of Rosalind breached the water. The creature regarded Wonder for a moment with dark eyes. The goat met her gaze unflinchingly, and after a moment, she inclined her head a fraction of an inch.

"Greetings, small one," she said in a rolling, musical voice. "I am Lady Beryl, queen of this domain. You are welcome here."

"Thank you, ma'am," said Wonder. He swept a bow, extending his foreleg and lowering his horns to the earth.

"Why have you come to see Old Beryl?"

"I want to know if there is any way to escape from the zoo," said Wonder. "The woman in the khaki shorts accidentally left my gate open, but now I cannot find a path to the outside. I . . . I want to leave this place . . . perhaps to go home but more likely to go on."

"Home," said Beryl heavily. "I have not seen my home in fifteen summers. If I knew the way out, wouldn't I have used it already?"

Wonder's head sagged as he asked aloud, "So is it hopeless then? Will I never see the ocean? Is mine really a future defined by a pen?"

Beryl swam closer, her large bulk cutting through the water with easy grace. She surfaced again, and this time, her face was inches from his, separated by only the mesh of the fence.

"What do you know of the ocean?" she asked, a strange edge to her voice.

"It was my quest to see it, ma'am," answered Wonder. "But I don't think I will ever get there now."

Beryl's eyes lost their focus as she gazed past Wonder. "The deeps are cool and dark," she said, "and filled with fishes to eat. The waves gallop towards the shore like mad, white-maned horses and crash in sprays of foam. The taste of salt was ever on my lips, while overhead the gray gulls circled, waiting for my scraps. I was queen of a kingdom once, ruler of both land and sea."

"What happened, Lady Beryl?"

"I was taken," she said. A twist of anger made her face seem almost monstrous. "The other sea lions watched as the men with nets and ropes dragged me from my throne. Now I am a queen in name only, a ruler in exile. Do you know what it is to be a queen without a realm to rule?

Beryl's eyes suddenly focused on Wonder once more. "These are old hurts, little one. Did you come here of a purpose to wound me with memories of the sea?"

"No," said Wonder hastily. "Ronan said that you might—"

"Ronan was wrong," Beryl answered. "There is no escape."

"But I must—"

Beryl opened her mouth very, very wide, displaying yellow teeth. "Leave me now, little goat. Unless you insist on seeing my fullness!"

Wonder did not need to be told twice. He turned tail and galloped away, unnerved by the sudden vehemence of Beryl's moods. Not knowing where else to go, he returned to his familiar enclosure. That night, as he slept fitfully, dreams of white-maned horses and giant sea lions filled his head.

39

JUMPING FENCES

THE NEXT MORNING, NONE OF THE OTHER ANIMALS EVEN RE-alized that Wonder had been outside of his pen. He told only Mac Craack about his adventure. The crow bobbed his head approvingly, but he also confirmed what Wonder had feared.

"No way out," he croaked. After a pause, he added, "Wonder wondering again. Good."

"I still want to see for myself," said Wonder.

Later that afternoon, one of the assistant keepers noticed the unlatched gate, frowned, and latched it securely. That was not, however, the end of Wonder's nighttime rambles. Although he knew now that beyond his pen was only a larger enclosure, he longed for new experiences. It took him many tries, but he finally mastered the art of leaping from an overturned bucket onto a barrel next to the fodder trough. From there, he was sure he could jump over the fence that surrounded his enclosure.

The nannies watched with wide, incurious eyes as he leaped and fell and leaped again all afternoon. "He's gone crazy, the poor thing," said Hazel, shaking her head sadly.

"Cracked as corn," agreed Lucinda.

"CRAACK," said Mac Craack, unable to help himself.

"Perhaps it's for the best that he did not want to mate after all," said Serena.

"Cheer up, Sere," said Hazel. "Come have some of this nice sweet hay."

"Oh yes, it *is* so nice and sweet," echoed Lucinda.

And with that, they lost interest in Wonder's antics.

Once more, the goat waited until nightfall to make his move. This time, Mac Craack accompanied him through the twisting, looping paths of Roca Plana, directing Wonder from the air as he had done so long ago on the journey through the mountains. When at last they reached what Mac Craack assured him was the edge of the zoo, Wonder found the way blocked by a great solid metal gate. It was more than three times his height and topped with a spiral of bright silver wire that the crow said was sharper than owl talons.

Wonder stared up at the gate for a long moment. He could not jump it. Here, then, was the border of his world.

"The only way out is through," said Wonder quietly. "But sometimes there *is* no way out."

A guttural sound emanated from Mac Craack. "Forgetful goat. Always a way. Always. Ay."

Wonder paused for a moment in response to the crow's comment.

Then, out of nowhere rose an anger that roared and twisted inside him. He ran pell-mell as though he could escape the anger if only he ran fast enough. He accelerated as he lowered his horns and rammed into the gate with all his might, bouncing off with an almighty crash. Wonder staggered, and prepared to run at the gate again.

Mac Craack fluttered into his path and spread his wings wide. His feathers glittered for a moment as if lit by a brilliant noonday sun, and their brightness made Wonder blink his eyes.

"Wonder is forget-full," said the crow with careful enunciation. "Light, Light. Into the Light. Through not through."

He turned the words into a kind of cackling, croaking song, and Wonder soon took up the chant. Once he felt calm enough to speak again, he said, "M.C., I have made a decision. I don't want to end up like bitter old Beryl, obsessed with the past and unable to let go of dead dreams."

Wonder looked back at the gate, which was barely dented from his effort.

"When she told me about her domain, it made me remember my old dream."

"Sea lion without sea is just lion," mused Mac Craack.

"It is driving her mad," said Wonder. "But the first lesson Oren taught me was that we are whatever is left when everything else is taken away. Beryl could not let go of her crown, but I can let go of my dream."

He turned from the gate and surveyed the sleeping zoo. There were dozens more enclosures he had never visited, dozens more souls to meet. Perhaps, if he were lucky, some of them would be Awake like him.

"I accept that I will not ever reach the ocean, M.C. But neither will I settle down with Serena and raise a family. I will stay here and be of service to the children who visit, and at night, I will find adventure. They can limit my body, but that is all."

As he said this, he felt a lifting of some of the shadows that had been threatening the heart of him. Now that he once more had a purpose, the tendrils of despair receded like mist in the breaking morning light. He had not realized how dark his thoughts had become until he turned once more into the Light. And in the Presence of the Light, the darkness slipped away.

Wonder and the crow returned to the enclosure to bed down for the night . . . only to find that there was no way for to him to get back in. The fence was too high without some stepping-stone to leap from. He was trapped outside.

With the fence looming, he remembered to go inside himself. On the third deep breath, as it passed through him like the wind itself, M.C.'s words suddenly fell upon him like a hammer. *Always a way. Through not through.* Clarity rose in him spontaneously.

The goat's chortle caused the crow to cock his head as he stared at Wonder with what was obviously a look of amusement.

"M.C., you are right. There is always a way."

With that, the goat rushed swiftly toward the enclosure. This time, though, free from the darkness that had weighed him down, he leaped. He soared just as he had so long ago when he first left his home paddock, and landed effortlessly.

He turned to gaze back at the fence, a curious look upon his face, not of surprise but of great interest. The crow landed beside him a moment later.

"I'm not trapped, M.C. I never was. And I never will be again."

"AWK, AWK, AWK," replied Mac Craack with obvious joy. "Full of wonder, Wonder-full."

40

THRIVING

WITH HIS NEWFOUND FREEDOM, WONDER'S LIFE CHANGED dramatically. Nights were spent exploring the far reaches of the zoo with Mac Craack. There was so much to see, and so much to discover. Afternoon naps became his routine since there was little sleep during the hours of darkness.

The change in him was significant as deep curiosity overcame what had formerly stifled him. Even the nannies noticed, with Serena one day saying she was happy he was finding such contentment at Roca Plana. When she or others asked about his comings and goings, he simply looked away.

While the zoo provided an endless stream of experiences, it was with the discovery of a large bird habitat that Wonder finally found what he'd been seeking. He'd passed it by a number of times before realizing that within the curving mesh walls, tropical birds slept. Very early one morning as was returning to the barn, he heard an abbreviated screech. He stopped, turned his head to listen, and studied what he now recognized was an enclosure largely covered by vines.

After some investigation, he realized the enclosure was designed to be viewed from inside. With further exploration, he found a small opening through the shrubs that allowed him to approach the mesh. When he did, he came nose to beak with a large, brilliantly colored bird whose eyes studied him carefully.

"Oh! Excuse me, Master Bird. I did not know what to expect, and yet there you are."

"Indeed, there I am, and you may want to refer to me as Madame," said a voice with an odd timbre. "Have you escaped from your pen?"

Wonder felt a lift of interest rise within him. "Yes, I have." He thought for a moment before adding. "Actually, I've recently learned it could not be otherwise." Then he chuffed in amusement. "My apologies as well. It did not occur to me you were female. That's embarrassing."

"Ahhh . . . ." said the bird. "I see you are Awake, my friend." The bird moved her head up and down as if to focus more clearly. "And how do you see yourself?"

"Well, my name is Wonder, but I am not that."

"Ark, ark!" she cackled. "You may call me Esperanza, or Espy if you prefer something simpler."

"Madame Espy, no offense intended, but what are you?"

The bird cocked her head as her beak opened and closed several times. Wonder had the impression Espy was carefully considering her response.

"They call me a scarlet macaw, but I am not that."

Wonder saw a twinkle of amusement in the bird's eyes, which he imagined was matched by a similar look in his own.

"Tell me more," urged the goat.

And with that, the macaw began to tell Wonder the story of her life. She'd been born in captivity, but there was a long tradition of wisdom with her kind, and so she had benefited from multiple teachers over the more than twenty years she had been alive.

"Regardless of this cage, there has always been a slow but steady flow of providers of knowledge," Espy added just as the light was breaking in the east. "And now, a mannered and Awakened goat has arrived to continue it. Just when you think you can no longer be surprised, life presents you with a surprise."

Wonder bowed to Espy in thanks. "I will return as often as I am able, Madame Espy."

"And I, dear Wonder, will very much look forward to it."

So began a conversation between the goat and the macaw that would last for many months. Before long, Mac Craack joined them. While the setting and dialogue were different, the feeling was very much like that of long ago when Wonder had spent hours with Oren and the crow, probing the nature of themselves and their world.

One afternoon as they rested in the shade, Awareness suddenly came to Wonder. "M.C., I could never have guessed how much I would find here at Roca Plana. Nothing is as it seems. Nothing."

41

Spring Blossoms

WONDER MET ESPY IN HIS FIRST WINTER AT ROCA PLANA. While not especially cold in this land far south of the mountains, it was cool enough that attendance at the zoo was much diminished. Wonder spent many long nights in the shelter of Espy's enclosure, where the thick walls of vines blocked most of the cold. He could not clearly identify how, but the macaw was deepening the goat's Awakening. Her good humor and the fascinating stories that had been passed down through generations of birds gave him a new perspective on the world and ways of being. It was a very gratifying experience, and it reminded him of much he had forgotten since being captured.

During the days, the zoo was very quiet, and Wonder found that he missed the laughing, running crowds of children. Mac Craack thought they were probably at school, and explained that school was a place where children were educated in the way of humans. The goat did not understand immediately until the crow described it as similar to the work Oren had done with him. That intrigued Wonder, but it puzzled him too.

"If they have these schools, then why aren't more humans Aware, M.C.?"

"CRAACK! Education not illumination."

"Hmmm. But Olivia is obviously Awake. Why is she different?"

"Listen goat, listen."

Though his conversations with Espy were re-Awakening Wonder to much of what he had come to know, he still lapsed into forgetting about inner guidance. Always, the crow reminded him with steady patience.

So he came back to the moment, dropping into the emptiness from which all things emanate. It took only a few breaths before clarity came.

"She was Awake before school. She remains Awake." He nodded thoughtfully. "I was Awake and remained Awake, even if I forgot for a little while." He glanced at Mac Craack.

"GRAWK!" announced the crow with a call that lingered in the air for long moments.

Wonder felt an urge to survey his surroundings as the call reverberated. He saw the earliest buds on the trees beneath an evanescent blue sky. His breath stilled of its own accord.

Then Wonder fell into the deepest Quiet he could imagine. He could hear the sounds of the breeze in the branches and the background rattle of the noises of Roca Plana, but the fleeting noise did not touch the inner Quiet. His eyes remained open, but he was somehow a distant observer as the veils parted. He had forgotten this sense of basking in the Presence, and he was awed by it.

The voice of Mac Craack was somewhere in that expansiveness. "GAW, GAW, GAW . . . Wonder works . . . working Wonder . . . ."

There was nothing, and yet there was everything. Wonder was still. Time was still. The depths of the Silence were overwhelming and yet deeply comforting. Wonder simply remained poised on the cusp of the wave of the now. *Breathe in. Breathe out. Breathe in. Breathe out. Breathe in. Breathe out.*

Time passed but timelessness reigned. A vision came to him. It was the image of the Tree of Light, though he knew that the fruit it bore was not material. It was life force itself. Every part of creation, every animal, every human, every thing was connected through this life, which was Presence itself. And the nature of Presence was in the Initiative that he had become aware of in the passage through the rocky canyon.

As if on cue, the words Oren had uttered just before Wonder departed played through his mind: *We are all part of Oneness. You and I will see each other again because Oneness never ceases, and we are long bonded within it.*

Wonder understood those words now in a deeper way than he had the first time he'd heard them. There was only One Life, only Presence itself, which makes itself known as Initiative, the creative force. And from the force springs every imaginable part of creation.

Into the Presence came a deep feeling of reverence, of awe. And the expansiveness became greater still. It was as if Wonder was for the first time seeing truly. It deeply humbled him that he could not see before this. Yet, he realized, you cannot see until you can see.

A deep breath rose within him as his eyes closed. He rested.

42

BEARING FRUIT

EVEN BEFORE HIS EYES OPENED, WONDER KNEW THE WORLD he was returning to would never be the same.

"GRAWK! One Goat?"

Wonder could not bear to open his eyes yet, so he spoke while holding close the lingering feelings.

"Do you know everything, M.C.?"

"GAW, GAW, GAW! All for One! One for all!"

"I'll take that as a yes," Wonder replied as he began to stretch before rising from the turf.

When he opened his eyes at last, the crow he saw shimmered for a moment before fading into a more-normal, mortal shape. Still, Mac Craack appeared larger, and his perfect feathers a deeper shade of blue-black.

Slowly the goat scanned the world beyond the crow, noticing how it looked more real than before. Everything he saw was some-how *more*, with crisper edges and richer colors.

Returning his attention to Mac Craack, he noted, "You are more perfected, M.C."

"See, see, see," gargled the crow.

Wonder began to laugh. Though silent, the laughter shook his body. The crow chuckled with him. There were simply no words or thoughts to communicate, just their shared moment of merriment.

A moment later Wonder noticed the nannies watching them strangely. Even they did not look the same to him, and a warmth and fondness for the silly, gossiping goats filled his chest. As he continued to look around the zoo, he saw everything as if for the first time.

And then he saw Olivia.

He was overwhelmed with feelings of joy and love. Seeing her now, for the first time since his eyes had become truly open, he could fully appreciate the joyful dance of color and light that was her spirit. He experienced something akin to déjà vu, as if he had seen Olivia's true nature before. But of course he hadn't, had he?

She had been true to her word to visit weekly, though never on the same day of the week. When she waved, he cantered to the fence.

Today she extended her hand with a strange brown fruit. "I realized you must surely get tired of apples. So I've brought you a pear. I wonder what you'll think of it."

Olivia's voice was like music to Wonder's ears. It had always been bright and lively, but today it was like a song. He studied her as he took a bite of the fruit. It had a firm texture and was sweet like an apple, but different.

She could see he enjoyed it, and she laughed with delight. Wonder wished he could tell her that it was not so much the fruit but her Presence that he enjoyed.

"You like it!" She giggled as she turned it for him to bite. "I brought more for your girls too. It's not fair to neglect them."

With that, she clucked her tongue as she extended her other hand with another pear. "Come on, ladies!"

Serena, Hazel, and Lucinda needed no urging. Wonder could hear them murmuring appreciatively as they approached.

"I always said she was a fine girl," said Hazel.

"No, you did not!'

"Did too!"

Their good-natured bickering faded into the background as Wonder simply stayed in the moment, watching Olivia. To her credit, she seemed comfortable being quiet, though the occasional cooing sound slipped from her as she fed and scratched their noses, heads, and necks.

As Wonder studied her, he could see the veil of the world go transparent once more. He could not figure out why she suddenly seemed so familiar to him. Of course, she had been visiting him for months at the zoo, but it was more than that. Then with a breath it was gone, and he imagined it was simply part of the continuing recognition of Oneness.

Olivia talked gently to all of them. She said nothing of particular importance to the nannies, and as she stood to go, her final words to Wonder were gentler still.

"I will see you as often as I can. Now I know to bring different fruit."

Then she was gone.

That night, Mac Craack joined Wonder and Espy. After recounting the entire experience, Wonder asked the macaw what she thought. After some contemplation, she spoke.

"Do you recall that on our first meeting, you said to me, 'There you are'?"

Wonder chortled. "I do. You replied, 'Indeed, there I am.' "

The macaw's beak opened and closed several times as her head jockeyed about. "Do you see now?"

Wonder drew himself into inner quiet and listened. An instant later, he let out a startled bleat as he understood.

"You meant there is only here and now. You know exactly what I'm describing, don't you?"

"Ah, dear goat, you become wiser and wiser. Yet I do not know the exact nature of your experience, any more than you can know mine. Each of us must tread the path in our own fashion. Yet it remains one path."

"Of course," Wonder said. "Of course."

Espy continued. "So you see, it is one experience, endlessly creative, an infinity of expressions. Still all one."

Mac Craack had been listening quietly until that moment but seemingly could no longer contain himself. "GRAACK! Here. There. Now."

Espy turned her white-rimmed eye on her fellow bird until he settled once more. "I do want to comment about M.C.'s growing perfection, which I too can see." The macaw bent her head left and right several times, and Wonder imagined it to be a kind of inner alignment demonstrated outwardly.

"Did you know that the original meaning of perfection has been misunderstood?" She paused a moment, and when Wonder did not answer, she continued. "It is now thought to mean without flaw. Yet its real meaning is well-suited-ness. To be a good fit for what lies ahead. For example, my fine plumage may seem rather garish in this drab enclosure, but the elders tell me I would blend in with the leaves, fruits, and flowers of the rainforest that is our ancestral home. And you, Wonder, are perfect for this sojourn of yours. While we may be without flaw in some final, ethereal sense, in the material world, it is more a matter of our ability to suit the purpose of our path."

Overhead, the pockmarked moon rose, and in the distance, the gibbons jabbered in their cages. Wonder, Mac Craack, and Espy lapsed into silence once more as the goat contemplated what it meant to be perfect in an imperfect world.

43

An Unexpected Blow

Wispy clouds feathered gently across a moon that loomed large in the night sky. Deep in thought, Wonder walked easily along the now well-known paths of Roca Plana. He had no destination in mind. Perhaps it was this contemplative state that somehow contributed to what ensued.

One moment he was uttering thoughts out loud, and glanced up toward the crow looming dark in the light of the moon. Suddenly he was stunned by a roar and a flash of motion at the periphery of his vision. A powerful blow sent Wonder tumbling. With breathtaking swiftness, his long-time protector dove from the sky.

Sprawled on the pavement outside a large barred enclosure, Wonder shook his head to clear the confusion. A quick mental scan told him he was only bruised. Then he turned his attention to the foreground—to the cage he'd wandered terrifyingly close to—where he saw a scattering of indigo feathers, and beyond them the crunching maw of a Bengal tiger bolting the crow down his gullet.

Wonder was crushed by the brutality of Mac Craack's death. Disbelief flooded through him. While it may have been his nature in addition to his name, never before had something been beyond his ability to even conceive. He blinked multiple times as he unsteadily lifted himself to his hooves.

A moment later, he was disembodied by shock, gazing down upon himself and the scene as if he were no longer present. This was not like the spiritual experiences of Awakening that brought with them a sense of elevation. Rather it was a blow of deep and profound trauma characterized by a seemingly numb indifference.

Though measured as an eternity, an instant later, a buzzing grew in his mind. He was so dislocated by it that he could not find himself. Even as a roar of rage burst inside him, he was struck nearly catatonic, and utterly alone with feelings that swamped him.

Wonder came to himself lying in the darkest corner of the barn as Serena hovered over him with obvious concern.

"What's wrong, Wonder?"

The goat cocked his head in an attempt to focus. A flood of despair swept over him. He was unable to respond and again collapsed into himself.

His next conscious awareness was of the zookeeper leaning over him flashing a tiny light alternatingly between his eyes. A thought arose. *Into the Light.* There was no energy in it, though, and it could not hold. Darkness descended once more.

44

From Darkness

WONDER WOULD NEVER BE ABLE TO EXPLAIN THE DEPTHS into which he fell. It was the great curiosity in Espy's eyes that registered next. There was no judgment, or even a concern, reflected there, only a deep, compassionate interest.

Suddenly Wonder was aware of breath rising in him. Then a pervasive sadness made itself known as a feeling radiating through him.

"There you are," squawked the macaw.

The goat blinked his eyes, then took several rather unbalanced breaths.

"Yes," he replied simply, though his voice sounded foreign to him. "How long has it been?"

"You have been missing for more than a week."

Wonder nodded. While it seemed there was much he ought to say, the need was simply insufficient.

"Thank you, Espy. I have much to consider."

He bowed deeply to the bird. "Thank you." Then he retreated to the barn.

As the sun rose, Wonder could not so easily evade the nannies. It was clear there had been much gossiping during the time since Mac Craack's death. From that came an endless series of questions from the girls, most of which went unanswered, though he was aware of a feeling of great patience toward their interests.

With winter again waning, the sun generated enough warmth for comfort while Wonder reflected day by day. His interactions with Espy lessened because there was so little to be said. Not that a great deal was not stirring, only that it did not lend itself to expression. So he breathed and listened inwardly.

Curiously, he did not miss Mac Craack. It was as if the Silence had Wonder.

Then one night, Wonder was struck from sleep only a short while after he had dozed off. What he heard himself say out loud was not something he had known, and he wasn't even sure he understood it when he said it. "There is no less Light in the darkness into which I fell."

Wonder puzzled over the thought, then began to deepen his breath as he fell into a deep, contemplative space unlike any he had before felt. He was intensely aware of the world around him, and yet somehow simultaneously aware of the state of his listening. And the space simply continued to hold as the night passed.

Only a short while before dawn, it finally released him. Wonder had never felt more alive or present. And he instantly knew it was time to speak to Espy.

He vaulted the fence easily and was soon beside the mesh in a whispered conversation with the macaw. Wonder recounted the entire experience, which was indelibly marked in his memory even if it was filled largely with nothing but a thoughtless expanse.

Espy nodded and nodded. When the goat had finished, she spoke simply. "You were being worked with very deeply, Wonder." The bird was quiet for a moment, then followed with a question. "And what do you make of it?"

Wonder chuckled as clarity came. "Mac Craack's death was perfect. It threw me outside myself in a way nothing else could. Only the greatest of blows could pierce the armor of me. And that dark place is now illuminated." He chortled again. "But not by Light. Awareness is the Light. Awareness sees beyond appearances. Darkness and Light are not separate, and one is not the cure for the other. There can be nothing without the contrast. When we finally see the whole, Awareness embodies both darkness and Light."

Then he suddenly began to weep.

"Oren knew. That's why he gave me the mantra. He knew *into the Light* would lead me beyond the Light." Wonder shook his head. "Nothing can take away Awareness, Espy. I am finally home . . . to myself. Wonder . . . not wonder."

After a long breath, he turned to Espy and bowed deeply.

Quickly the bird interjected. "Wonder, how is it this terrible loss has passed through you?"

"I cannot say, my friend. Yet it seems that all things are made right when deep in Awareness." He shook his head. "Who can explain the mystery?" After a long silence, Wonder concluded, "I must go now, Espy. The day is at hand."

That same afternoon, Olivia came bearing sweet fruits like little purple orbs. Somehow Wonder was not surprised when she uttered familiar words.

"There you are." Then with a light touch to his forehead, she added, "I was very worried about you."

45

CHILDREN AND MORE

WITH THE PASSAGE OF TIME CAME CHILDREN, IN FAR GREATER numbers than had ever visited him before. Espy said they were drawn to the Light that increasingly emanated from him. While that was a pleasant thought, Wonder was very aware of the unique Presence each child carried within. Over and over again, he was made aware of the Tree of Light through them. They came in endless forms, with every conceivable demeanor. Some were tall and slender, others short and plump. Some were meek and mild, while other whooped and ran like wild things. They were all a demonstration of Oneness. Wonder simply entered into the moment with each and every one.

Olivia visited more frequently, but she was often hard pressed to spend much time with Wonder because of the growing number of children clamoring to be near him. She would simply slide down the fence and feed the nannies an ever-changing variety of fruit.

Wonder was absorbed into the interactions with the children, and increasingly the adults. Some nights, he would meet Espy and share observations. On occasion, the absence of Mac Craack added a bittersweet quality. He never avoided the feelings, but they always left a tinge of sadness upon him.

One day brought a very strange little boy who would not release his father's hand. The boy was without the animation the other children displayed, and he did not speak at all. Regardless, his eyes were alive.

When there was a break in the flow of people, Wonder made extended eye contact with the boy. Stillness descended upon them, and after a long moment, the child smiled, then pointed at him. His father was surprised and led his son closer.

The boy's extended finger touched the goat's nose and rested there lightly. Wonder maintained eye contact and breathed with him. When their connection was broken by the arrival of a rowdy group of children, Wonder knew there had been a change in the boy.

When he discussed it with the macaw that evening, Espy repeated, "Here. There. Now." Then she offered a possible translation. "Wonder, do you suppose something happens when we come together in the Presence?"

The goat's head cocked as he considered the thought with long steady breaths. "If there is only Oneness, and it only exists in the moment, why not?"

As he heard it, he imagined the crow's raucous cry splitting the air with pleasure, "GRAACK!"

It was only at dawn the next day, in the thin, restless moments between sleeping and waking, that he was shaken awake by the returning vision of the Tree of Light. What he sensed defied words, but it was clear that Espy's suggestion was true.

In the Presence, in the now, matters are not just right. They can be made right. That is the true nature of Illumination.

Wonder vowed that morning to welcome as many children as possible—and, if they could be still and attentive, their parents as well—into the quiet shelter of Presence. Days gave way to weeks and then years. As seasons passed, the richness of his experiences only increased, often to the point of being indescribable.

There were more and more children, and with them, more and more adults. During one winter, the people in khakis moved the goats for a time. When they returned, the paddock had been enlarged, and there were two barns. Before long, more goats arrived, and Wonder greeted them politely. None were Awake, but they were pleasant enough and got along well with Serena, Lucinda, and Hazel. Two of the goats were nannies, barely older than kids, but the third was a buck with a fine copper coat. It wasn't long before Serena started giving him the kind of sidelong glances she'd once given Wonder, but this time, they were returned with equal interest.

A few weeks after the expansion, the frizzy-haired zookeeper, who had taken to visiting with Wonder in the evening before she went home, leaned against the fence and mopped her ruddy face with her handkerchief. "Who knew kids liked goats so much, huh? You're more popular than the elephants, mister billy goat."

She paused thoughtfully. "But hey, I keep coming back here too. You're something else," she said, and slipped a biscuit through the bars of the fence for Wonder to eat.

Then one morning, many seasons after Wonder had first come to Roca Plana, Hazel did not wake up. Serena and Lucinda bleated in distress, and Wonder did his best to calm the nannies. This too was part of the Tree of Light. Some things changed and some things didn't.

One day, a contingent of men and women arrived with equipment Wonder did not understand. There was a great hubbub, and the goat was posed in a variety of ways. Espy explained later that they were reporters for the local news media, a gossip network for humans, and that he was the focus of a story. It seemed that word of his popularity had spread beyond the zoo.

The goat only marveled at it all.

Wonder grew fatter from all the biscuits and Olivia's fruit, despite his nightly treks through the zoo. Over time, he collected a great range of experiences.

On another day, a large cat tried to lure him into striking distance. Wonder could not imagine that so powerful a creature could possess such an alluring voice. Yet the image of Mac Craack's demise was not forgotten, and he steered clear. Afterward, he was surprised that there was not even a trace of bitterness within him. It had been lifted from him.

There were countless attempts to make greater connection with other creatures. Communicating with the peacocks proved them to be nothing but beautiful emptiness. Every now and again, he would try to teach the Kevins to find their inner calm, but nothing seemed to undo their fainting spells. He steered clear of Beryl, but he found the bears to be fine company even though they were not nearly so Awake as Boboso had been. The prairie dog community proved to be entertaining with the residents' endless antics, and the armadillo family was as strange as anything Wonder had seen in his many long years.

Olivia grew into a slender and gracious young woman. Her attention to him never waned. She was a source of never-ending pleasure for Wonder, yet also a cause for much curiosity. Wonder scoffed at Espy's suggestion that she was his soul mate. With the passage of time and the deepening of their connection, however, he contemplated the bond of love and understanding between them, a bond that did not need words. There was only Presence when Olivia visited.

46

THE FULLNESS OF TIME

ONE SPRING, MANY YEARS LATER, WONDER FOUND HIMSELF once again in a metal container on wheels. The morning had begun with what he thought was a routine trip through the tunnels to the room where he was regularly examined. Instead, the woman in khakis took him through a set of large doors that were entirely unfamiliar. Before long, they arrived at a ramp. She patted him very kindly before handing the rope to a gentle young man who coaxed him up the plank.

Wonder would always remember the break in the zookeeper's voice when she said, "Goodbye, my dear little friend." His final memory of Roca Plana would be her curious sadness, paired with the call of one of the peacocks splitting the early morning quiet.

As the box lurched forward, Wonder was aware of the absence of fear or regret, which he thought quite odd. So he lapsed into inner stillness to probe and inquire.

Once again, my curiosity has trumped any concern for myself. Still, this is the first trek in a very long time that Mac Craack has missed. It is unfortunate I was not able to say goodbye to Espy and Serena and the others, but they will be fine without me.

Then Wonder thought of Olivia, and an ache pierced through him. He had seen her only a few days before. She had seemed particularly animated and had fed him tiny little berries one by one. His thoughts scrolled back trying to recall her words, but his attention had wandered, as it did more and more often these days, and he remembered only the shape of his feelings and not the particulars of her visit.

On another day, he had visited otters. While they were not Awake like Lydia, they were the liveliest of all the creatures at Roca Plana. Wonder had watched them for a long time, remembering the Waters of the Otters and the golden afternoon he'd spent with Lydia and her brother, as well as Jessie and Jimbob. He wondered what name the male kit had eventually taken.

That night, Lydia appeared in his dream. There had been an especially bright light in her eyes, which he fell into in the dream. It felt like coming home.

I wonder if this is the end for me? This is how goats disappeared back at the farm.

With that, a tendril of fear arose from deep within Wonder's gut. He noticed it and began to breathe into it.

Into the Light. Into the Light. For even darkness is of the Light.

The depths of his meditations were such that he lost track of the ride. Every now and again, a bump or a thump would intrude, but it would immediately recede from the Presence.

After a time that was as long as it was, the movement ceased. Wonder barely noticed, so deep was he in the quiet stillness. It was only with the crash of the ramp to the ground that he was drawn back into the world. With his return came a scent he had never known before, though it reminded him a little of the salt lick that was kept for the deer at Roca Plana. It blew upon the breeze sweeping in through the now-open door. Wonder turned and blinked as sunshine filtered into the darkness. Then at the gentle urging of the young man, he stepped toward the ramp with senses engaged. There was nowhere but here and now.

As he came fully into the warmth of the sun, Wonder blinked for a few moments in confusion. Where was he? And why had he been brought to this place? Then delight rose in him when he saw Olivia beaming and smiling. To the right beyond her, grassland swept gently downward. And farther beyond the waving stalks of grass, an expanse of blue disappeared into the horizon.

He was stunned. It was the ocean that Wonder had smelled. Nothing could have prepared him for the experience. He drank it in and was filled.

With that fulfillment, his attention was drawn to his left by a tug of Awareness. There stood a smallish, mottle-coated female goat studying him impassively.

As soon as Wonder saw her, he softened his senses to explore this surprising development. After a few breaths, he knew there was a reason for her arrival.

Wonder had the distinct impression she was feeling him out with her own Awareness. He noticed her noticing.

With sudden insight, he knew she would be his student. A deep feeling of pleasure coursed through him. It was one of the most important things that had not yet come to him. He dipped his nose to acknowledge her. She responded in kind.

As he trotted down the ramp, he heard once more a raucous call. "GRAWWK! Wonder full?"

Against all reason, Mac Craack soared overhead. Wonder watched him fly with amazement and amusement.

Into the Light, whispered Presence.

Epilogue

BEYOND WONDER

THERE IS A PLACE OUTSIDE OF TIME AND BEYOND SPACE. Wonder had sometimes found it in his dreams and deep in the heart of the Quiet. Here he was no longer a white goat. In fact, he was not a goat at all.

My name is Wonder, but I am not that, he thought with amusement.

"Greetings, Wonder-not-Wonder," croaked a familiar voice. Before him appeared a glimmering form, shot through with splinters of rainbow, that Wonder knew at once to be Mac Craack's true essence. The Light of his being pulsed and spiraled in an endless dance, and it occurred to Wonder that he too might look as M.C. did in this place.

"You're beautiful!" Wonder exclaimed. "Why did you choose to be a windblown, one-eyed crow for all those years when you were so vast and bright inside?"

Although he could not see it, he felt Mac Craack's wry gaze and knew that even here, answers would not be freely given. Wonder considered Mac Craack's miraculous transformations over the course of their journey together, from the ragged bird who had saved him from the owl to the glossy, sleek companion in his adventures to the white-feathered, flawless bird that had emerged from the snow on the slopes of the mountain. Even the crow that had been killed and devoured. They were all Mac Craack, and at the same time, none of them were Mac Craack. Just as Wonder had once been a fleecy white kid and then a strong young buck and finally a venerable goat, and now this formless Wonder.

"What you are," said Wonder, recalling Master Oren's words as clearly as if he'd heard them only yesterday, "is what is left when that which is not you is cast aside."

"So you *were* listening, little one," sounded a voice that could only be Oren's.

Wonder's spirit thrilled at the sound of his teacher's words. It was a sound he had not thought to hear again, but in this place, all things were possible, and beautiful, and true.

"Master Oren!" he cried. Had he been able, Wonder would have scampered and frisked like a kid in spring grasses. Oren's form was also made of coruscating light, but Wonder somehow instantly recognized his old teacher.

It seemed like he ought to have many, many questions for his two teachers, and yet as he settled into this formless self, knowingness was his nature. "Ha!" he bleated. "All that practice, here realized." With that, there was nothing to do but embrace and share this space with Oren and Mac Craack.

Wonder became aware that a review of his life on Earth was in the order of things. In an instant, or even less, he felt a protected space form around him and his teachers. He imagined it to be an energetic bubble that held them.

Impressions of his incarnation as Wonder the goat slowly rose and fell, not as a chronology but as related concepts and themes. First came learning images.

"I was a student first and foremost," he heard himself affirm.

Oren's voice echoed with gravitas, "Yes, you were, dear Wonder. You filled that role marvelously well."

Then came a series of risky and sometimes comical adventures. A curious sense arose in Wonder as the visions cycled before him. "I was lucky I didn't die! Very lucky," he added with some humility. "I was so . . . so . . . attached to the identity of wandering and adventuring," he said. "It gave me meaning since the very first time my father suggested it was a virtue."

"CAW! CAW! No goat, no Wonder. No Wonder no goat."

"Of course," replied Wonder. "It served me well."

With that there came a parade of those who had played a role in the tale of Wonder the goat, every creature great and small. There was Boboso, and Espy, and even old Manuel and bitter Beryl. Among the living creatures were other things too, the settings and circumstances of his adventures. He saw the old barnyard, and the canyon where he had encountered the coyotes, and the rocks he had so carefully and laboriously climbed. All these had formed and shaped the life he'd lived. Everything, absolutely everything was part of his path. Then Mac Craack's death scene replayed, yet it was devoid of all horror. In truth, it was nothing.

He was dumbfounded by the beauty of the design that had guided and supported him his entire life as Wonder. With that Awareness, everything in the moment suddenly suffused into a massive, brilliantly shimmering Tree of Light that hung in the air. Nothing was omitted. Nothing could be omitted. And all of it . . . all of it was for his benefit. No exceptions.

The silence that welled up then was so profound that he could never have borne it while in earthly form. The allness of it simply held and pulsed.

Into that space rang the gargled voice of perfect crowness. "AWE. AWE. AWE." The last word rang like a bell for longer than long, only ending when another impression emerged.

Wonder experienced the long, fulfilling time that had begun when he arrived at the ranch by the ocean. Scenes cascaded, settings of golden grasslands, mists from the sea, bluffs above crashing waters, crystalline nights and amber mornings, and the seasons that came and went, came and went. All these were the realization of the vision of the sea that had called him from somewhere deep within.

Almost magically, the relevance of his student and their work together revealed itself. Wonder recalled the first words he had heard the she-goat utter, a phrase she would repeat over and over through the years. "Well, isn't this interesting." The parallel to his own tendencies toward curiosity was uncanny, which provided the foundation for a fine relationship between them.

With a flash of clarity, he recalled she was named Butterfly, and that teaching her had cemented his own learning. Whatever his future held, it would be at a level greatly advanced by that learning. Still more gratitude flooded Wonder. Teaching proved to be inseparable from learning. We could not do it alone.

Espy's words dropped into his thoughts. "Just when you think you can no longer be surprised, life presents you with a surprise."

And throughout the entire replay of his experience, there was Olivia. At last, long after he had given up his dream, Olivia had brought him to her house by the sea, where he spent the final years of life plucking fruits from her palm and bearing the attention of her two young children as well as an old goat could.

Now that he had passed beyond physical form, Wonder could finally see the thing that had eluded him in life. As Olivia's dancing eyes lingered, they changed and shifted until they became the playful, inquisitive essence of Lydia the otter. They were one and the same. The form was irrelevant; the bond between them endured. Wonder wept with joy and still more surprise. Even though breathing was apparently not needed in this place, he felt the breath of life coursing through him. He knew he would see her again, as surely as he knew that they had walked the path together before in a hundred different forms.

"Know now?" asked Mac Craack.

"Oh, yes, M.C. Oh, yes."

Wonder rested then, in silent timelessness.

Slowly, ever so slowly, a deep resonant voice formed in the allness. It was one voice, but Wonder knew beyond doubt it was also the voice of all his teachers and guides along the journey of his life. *Of course, it would be a single voice; there is only One.*

"Are you yet willing?" it asked with weight and depth.

Another deep breath pressed through him. This time it was the breath of animation returning to form. The adventure was to begin anew.

AFTERWORD

THE STORY OF WONDER BECAME CLEAR TO ME ON THE HEELS of a conversation with my sister. I remember her words exactly, "No one ever went to their grave wishing they had worked another day."

In an instant, I knew that comment was false for me. I love the work I do in the world, a part of which is telling stories to help people understand.

And just as fast as that thought dissolved, I realized there were several stories I must tell before I pass from the Earth. The first was my novel, *A Killer's Grace*. The second is Wonder's story. Of course, there are a few more yet to tell.

This story would never have been possible without some very important people. For Natalie and Brianne, my daughters to whom Wonder is dedicated, I am deeply appreciative for a love I do not comprehend.

There are a handful of teachers who have worked with me in ways that allow such a story as this to arise through me. To Sam Dement, Patrick Kurp, Patricia O'Gorman, Tom Selby, and Judy Borich: I can never say thank you enough for helping me overcome myself. For Joel Goldsmith and George Gurdjieff, who yet live beyond form, thank you for the wisdom you imparted into the world. It has helped me immensely. Erin Elizabeth Long gave me a mighty jumpstart when I was stalled. Donna Cooley Long, Al Cotton, and Mari Selby played integral roles in bringing this story to market. A number of friends provided many, many corrections and suggestions.

These thoughts would be immaterial if Wonder himself had not found me. I do not know from whence he came, nor to what end. Yet I love that goat.

So too have I come to love Mac Craack. If all stories are ultimately biographical, the crow demonstrates my spiritual aspirations—all of which has spawned a phrase that has long served me as a mantra: "Look for signs of Wonder in the world."

So it is. And so it shall be.

THE LIGHT AND THE SHADOW: TWO TALES OF INNOCENCE

THE STORY IN THIS BOOK AND THE ONE IN A KILLER'S GRACE are like bookends in one of the most important learnings of my life. Much of my time now is spent working with people who need to forgive and to heal. From that work has come an understanding of inherent innocence, which is a subject I will be exploring more fully in coming books. Regardless, if *A Killer's Grace* represents the darkness of the path to innocence, *My Name Is Wonder* is the lightness of that same path. One is yin and the other is yang, two sides of a truth and reality that cannot be separated. As a good friend says, "Damn it, you can't just take the good stuff and call it Grace!" I cannot disagree. And I am certain that innocence is our destination—or, if you prefer, it is with us all the while, awaiting our awakening to it.

To purchase *A Killer's Grace,* visit your local independent bookstore or any online bookseller.

—Ronald Chapman

ABOUT THE AUTHOR

Ronald Chapman has followed many paths of spiritual and religious study over the past thirty years. As a workshop leader and motivational speaker, he has shown countless people how Seeing True,™ his signature practice, can produce extraordinary changes in their lives.

Chapman is one of only sixty-eight International Accredited Speakers recognized by Toastmasters International. He is the author of the novel *A Killer's Grace* and the inspirational books *Seeing True: Ninety Contemplations in Ninety Days* and *What a Wonderful World: Seeing Through New Eyes*. In 2015 and 2016, Ozark Mountain Publishing released audio sets that complement his writings. *Breathing, Releasing and Breaking Through: Practice for Seeing True* explores the use of breathwork and meditation to promote inner healing. *Seeing True: The Way of Spirit* presents a psycho-spiritual philosophy and practices for transforming what and how we see.

You can learn more about his transformational philosophy at www.SeeingTrue.com, and about its application to twelve-step recovery at www.ProgressiveRecovery.org. For more information about Chapman's entire portfolio, visit: www.RonaldChapman.com.

Made in the USA
San Bernardino, CA
17 July 2016